Group's

EMERGENCY RESPONSE
HANDBOOK

for **SMALL GROUP LEADERS**

Loveland, Colorado

www.group.com

Group resources actually work!

This Group resource helps you focus on **"The 1 Thing"**— a life-changing relationship with Jesus Christ. "The 1 Thing" incorporates our **R.E.A.L.** approach to ministry. It reinforces a growing friendship with Jesus, encourages long-term learning, and results in life transformation, because it's:

Relational
Learner-to-learner interaction enhances learning and builds Christian friendships.

Experiential
What learners experience through discussion and action sticks with them up to 9 times longer than what they simply hear or read.

Applicable
The aim of Christian education is to equip learners to be both hearers and doers of God's Word.

Learner-based
Learners understand and retain more when the learning process takes into consideration how they learn best.

Visit our Web site: **www.group.com**

Credits
Contributors: Rev. Dr. L.H. Chamberlain, Jr.; Linda Crawford; Kelly M. Flanagan, Ph.D.; Kelly Schimmel Flanagan, Ph.D.; Kate S. Holburn; Rev. Dr. John C. Jorden; Rebekah Knight-Baughman, Ph.D.; Joy-Elizabeth F. Lawrence; James W. Miller; A. Koshy Muthalaly, Ph.D.; Summer Rivers Salomonsen; Carl Simmons; Trevor Simpson; Amber Van Schooneveld; Terri S. Watson, Psy.D.; and Amy Weaver
Editor: Roxanne Wieman
Creative Development Editor: Matt Lockhart
Chief Creative Officer: Joani Schultz
Assistant Editor: Amber Van Schooneveld
Book Designer/Print Production Artist: Pamela Poll Design
Cover Art Director/ Designer: Jeff A. Storm
Illustrator: Pamela Poll
Production Manager: Peggy Naylor

Unless otherwise indicated, all Scripture quotations are taken from the *Holy Bible*, New Living Translation, copyright © 1996, 2004. Used by permission of Tyndale House Publishers, Inc., Wheaton, Illinois 60189. All rights reserved.

Library of Congress Cataloging-in-Publication Data
Group's emergency response handbook for small group leaders / [contributors, L.H. Chamberlain, Jr. ... et al.].
    p. cm.
  ISBN-13: 978-0-7644-3181-4 (pbk. : alk. paper)
  1. Church group work–Handbooks, manuals, etc. 2. Small groups–Religious aspects–Christianity–Handbooks, manuals, etc. 3. Suffering–Religious aspects–Christianity–Handbooks, manuals, etc. 4. Pastoral care–Handbooks, manuals, etc. I. Chamberlain, L. H. II. Title: Emergency response handbook for small group leaders.
  BV652.2.G695 2006
  253'.7–dc22
                                        2006009753
ISBN 0-7644-3181-1
10 9 8 7 6 5 4 3 2   15 14 13 12 11 10 09 08 07 06
Printed in the United States of America.

Contents

Introduction

It's not easy losing a spouse. Or dealing with depression. Or facing down an addiction. It's hard and painful and brutal.

But it doesn't have to be lonely.

Christians should never have to face trials on their own. Those around them—their Christian brothers and sisters—should rise up and support them.

"Share each other's burdens, and in this way obey the law of Christ" (Galatians 6:2).

Although it isn't easy going through trials, it's also tough being on the outside and trying to help those who are suffering.

You don't know what to do. You're worried about hurting their feelings or stepping on their toes or saying the exact *wrong* thing.

Of course you care—you love them! It isn't that you don't want to help—it's just that you don't know how.

Group's Emergency Response Handbook will help you come alongside those in your small group who are facing tough times. From care and counseling tips, to practical ideas for your small group, to what to say and what not to say, this book offers insight after insight into how to care for the hurting.

Of course, it'd be great if you never had to pick up this book! But the reality is that everyone faces tough times—including the people in your small group. And they need your help.

So when someone you love is going through a divorce, dealing with a rebellious child, or considering suicide…it's time to pick up this guide. Use the table of contents to find the specific hurt for which you're caring, and then flip to that section.

Once there, you'll find a **real life narrative**—a story from someone who's been there. Sometimes they're inspiring, and you'll read how the support and love of a small group sustained someone through a hard time. Other times they're disappointing and tell stories of people left alone during tragedy or rejected during trial. Either way, these stories will move you, and they'll show you the importance of devoted friends.

Each section also includes **care and counseling tips** that will give you practical ideas for reaching out in love. From baking dinner, to mediating in arguments, to intentional reminiscing, these ideas will help you effectively support the hurting people in your small group.

Next, you'll find **group tips** for your whole small group. These practical ideas will help your entire group support the hurting member during his or her trial.

And, finally, you'll find an invaluable section on **what to say and what not to say** to your friend. The words we use can help or hurt a friend more than we know. This section will help you avoid the hurtful comments and use the helpful ones.

You'll also find useful boxes in each section that offer Scripture help, guidelines for referring your friend to a professional counselor, and additional resources, such as books and Web sites, that you can use as you support your hurting friend.

Our prayer for this book is that it will help you help a friend during a difficult time.

> *"He comforts us in all our troubles so that we can comfort others. When they are troubled, we will be able to give them the same comfort God has given us"* (2 Corinthians 1:4).

The Death of a Child
Supporting Parents Through the Tragedy

with counseling insights from **REV. DR. JOHN C. JORDEN**
+ ministry tips from **KATE S. HOLBURN**

Several years into their marriage, Sean and Victoria experienced unbelievable joy when their son, Nathan, was born...then unbelievable pain when they lost him. Here is their story.

Emergency Response Handbook: *What was your family and church situation like at the time?*

Victoria: We were 27 and 28 with an 18-month-old daughter. Our church was small—about 120 people—and we were involved as ministry leaders.

Sean: About seven months into her pregnancy, Victoria woke in pain; she was in preterm labor at 34 weeks. The baby was transverse in the womb and couldn't be delivered, so they did an emergency C-section. And there was our son, Nathan—whom we were so incredibly thrilled to meet. He spent two weeks in an oxygen tent in the nursery. My mother came to help, but no one from the church ever came.

ERH: *What happened after you brought Nathan home?*

Victoria: We brought Nathan when he reached five pounds. One day after about a week, he started crying and wouldn't stop. Sean was at work with our only car, and in those pre-cell phone days, I couldn't reach him. I felt alone and didn't know who to turn to, but finally convinced a close acquaintance from church to drive us to the hospital.

At the hospital, it was chaos. The sense of the out-of-control… everything was happening so fast. They flew Nathan to another hospital by helicopter.

Sean: After more tests, the doctors told us that it was bacterial meningitis.

ERH: *What were the days that followed like for you?*

Victoria: We were at that hospital for six total days. We called our pastor once, and that was the only interaction we had with anyone from church. We didn't hear from anybody else. Yet we were completely unafraid. There was no doubt in our minds that Nathan would be healed. What a miraculous story it would make!

ERH: *What happened next?*

Sean: The doctor came and told us the news…Nathan was not going to be healed. That was when we had our first breakdown. We lost all physical strength and collapsed to the floor in broken grief.

Victoria: We made the devastating decision to take Nathan off the ventilator and signed the "Do Not Resuscitate" form. They disconnected Nathan's oxygen and left us alone with him. We held him and sang and talked to him as he faded. After a while we noticed that he was fighting to breathe in response to our voices. We didn't want to prolong his struggle, so we fell silent and waited. Afterward, we walked out into the dark parking garage. It was 3:00 a.m., and the realization hit us that nobody knew what had happened. No one was there to drive us home; no one was waiting at home with a quiet hug and a meal.

ERH: *What response did you get from your church after Nathan's death?*

Sean: Not knowing what else to do, people gave us advice and spiritual counsel. They had good intentions, but the words seemed harsh and minimizing. Some people simply avoided the subject altogether. They probably believed it would be better for us if we never talked about what happened or heard Nathan's name. Or at least it would be easier for them. People desperately wanted us to be the strong, well-adjusted, happy couple we'd been before.

Victoria: We felt isolated and abandoned, but, so no one would feel uncomfortable, we played the same game...not bringing Nathan up in conversation, putting on fake smiles, saying we were fine. We should have thought it was strange how little care we got. But there's no way to know how it's supposed to be. Only later did we realize what we were missing.

ERH: *What kind of needed support did you receive?*

Victoria: Two things stand out. First, a couple of friends bought Nathan's cemetery plot for us. It was a thoughtful gesture, and it took a practical burden off our shoulders. Also, a non-church friend came to me one day, enfolded me in a hug, and didn't say a single word. In that hug, I felt loved and understood.

ERH: *What was the impact on your marriage and your involvement in church?*

Sean: We started living parallel lives in our marriage—not fighting, but not connecting either. And because we weren't involved with each other and didn't have emotional or spiritual care from the church, we were also disconnected from God. We didn't pray together or open our Bibles for a long time. We were confused, disengaged. But we were never angry at anyone or God.

Victoria: We went right back to church after Nathan's death, but never recovered with the church, and we left after a year. It was only when we moved to another state for Sean's new job that we began to experience the richness of God's healing...and found the warm, living sanctuary we had been missing in a church body. We met people who loved and cared, listened and laughed.

ERH: *How does your and Nathan's story continue?*

Sean: We mark every one of his birthdays and talk about him often, both within our family and among close friends. And now, in God's timing, we can recognize the impact Nathan's life has had. For example, through the memorial service, a man committed to a faith relationship in Jesus.

Victoria: We'll always live with grief, but by God's grace, we have people to carry that burden with us—and help celebrate our son's beautiful life.

Care and Counseling Tips

THE BASICS

+ Death comes to your group. The death of a child.

A grieving father once asked how anyone could survive the thunderbolt that was the death of his child. For that father, and for so many who have lost a child, the painful answer is this: "We do survive—that's the problem!"

While all death is difficult, the very nature of the death of a child is traumatic, and it's a common understanding in grief literature that traumatic death is more difficult to grieve than non-traumatic death. It lasts longer and hurts more deeply.

Wally's son was murdered in a botched computer store robbery. Fred was an innocent clerk who happened to recognize one of the thieves. Since that time, Wally has divided his own life into "the good time before Fred's death and the bad time since." The death has become the watershed of his life perspective. The normal acute phase for grief in the death of a child is *two* to *seven* years. The pain may not be as intense for the whole time, but it does linger intently. And the loss will stay with the parents for a lifetime.

Victoria died at age 98. She was somewhat of a recluse and had no known family. Her "valuables" were in a lockbox at the bank. They consisted of a worn teddy bear and a picture of her infant daughter who had died at age 1 some 80 years earlier.

It never goes away.

Care Tips

+ Come right away!

Don't assume someone else will go to the grieving parents—it's not always the case. As soon as you hear about the death, drop what you're doing, and go to the parents. Nothing shows love more than your presence.

+ Stay.

Parents in grief sometimes can't stand being in their own skin. Your willingness to sit with them is a promise of hope and love. Stay as long as you can, and when you have to leave, try to coordinate for someone else from your church or small group to be there. Be receptive to the parents' need to be alone, but don't leave until they request you do so. Stop by regularly—especially in the first few months after the tragedy.

+ Acknowledge that grief is physical.

Grief is as much a physical experience as an emotional one. Your friends will be exhausted, and yet they'll have trouble sleeping. Their immune system will be depleted—they may get more colds.

Encourage your friends to rest, to drink lots of water, and eat regularly. Bring the parents food or invite them to your house to share a meal.

+ Help with the little things.

Funeral arrangements. Death certificate. Calling family and friends. Notifying the school. All things that must be done...but overwhelming details for parents in grief. Help as you can.

Don't wait for your friends to ask for help.

Speak up. Talk directly to them. Wounded and grieving parents have little energy, and the fewer times they have to reach out for help, the better. Be there for them. Do they need a meal? Baby-sitting? A night out? Someone to clean their house? Make the offer.

+ Pray with them and for them.

Grieving parents may or may not be prepared to trust God. Don't judge them or preach at them. Be ready and willing to respond to their questions regarding faith and what you believe. In allowing them to speak up first, you let them set the pace, not you. In the meantime, offer simple prayers and reminders of God's presence.

+ Stick around.

Grieving for a child is a process. Don't expect it to be over in a week, a month, a year. Continue to offer your support and love through the long haul—even when it seems as if they no longer need it. Grief for a child can resurface again and again in a lifetime. Make sure your friends know that they can call you when it happens.

WHEN TO REFER

It's always a good idea to refer a grieving parent to a professional grief counselor. Most parents will benefit from this experience, and it will help them move more quickly through the grieving process. However, in the following instances, it's *necessary* to seek professional help:

+ **The person has stopped eating or sleeping.**
+ **The person doesn't leave the home for an abnormal period of time.**
+ **The person is unable to attend to surviving children.**
+ **The person shows signs of suicidal intent (see** *Chapter 4—Suicide***).**

A support group for grieving parents may also be a good option for your friends.

Counseling Tips

Most parents who lose a child will benefit from seeing a professional counselor. While the following counseling tips may help as you minister to your friends, don't hesitate to suggest they pursue a grief counselor as well.

+ Familiarize yourself with the stages of grief.

See *Chapter 2—The Death of a Spouse.* These stages, though usually present, are often stronger and more prolonged in the instance of a child's death. Don't expect your friends to go through the stages in a precise order—they may go back and forth or skip a stage. Support your friends during each stage of grief.

+ Don't judge your friends' denial or try to force reality on them.

Shock or numbness will usually follow the death of a child. This is a normal coping mechanism and shouldn't cause you to worry. The death of a child is a powerful emotional event. There's no way that most parents can quickly get their minds around this reality...and all the ramifications of it. Denial doesn't mean your friends don't "know" their child is dead—it simply means they can't immediately take in the full meaning of what has happened.

The best thing you can do for your friends during this stage is to simply be there. Be silent. Pray. Share in their laughter and tears. Hold them.

+ Be there during the hardest times.

Once the funeral is over, reality will start to set in, and your friends will have to face an unbearable pain. Most parents who lose a child will have a hard time sleeping, eating, and doing the everyday things that are necessary to survive. The pain is simply too overwhelming to function. Many describe it as a pain within the chest and the gut or a longing in the head. One mother said it was as if her chest was always on fire and nothing would put out the flame.

During this phase, many grieving parents will look and search for their child. They'll walk into crowds with a keen, alert eye, hoping that maybe, just maybe, the child might be there. A fleeting glance, a similar body frame triggers a memory and a hope—maybe it didn't really happen; maybe it was a mistake.

During these times, it's critical that you be there for your friends…and that you don't judge them. Don't criticize them for an unclean house. Don't rush them through grief. Don't chastise them for holding on to hope.

Do encourage them to see a professional grief counselor during this time. Do offer to help them with the everyday chores and necessities. Do invite them to social functions. Do talk regularly with them about their child and the death.

+ Help parents feel normal in their abnormal situation.

The death of a child taxes all one's emotional resources. Nothing is normal. Many parents who have lost a child will say they feel as if they're "going crazy." Listen to their stories, and keep judgments to yourself. Some of the things they tell you may indeed seem crazy to you. But more than likely, they are *normal* and *expected* responses to the death of a child. There are parents who report sitting in the child's closet, smelling his clothes to capture "his smell." Other parents have worn a piece of their child's garments, talked regularly to their dead child, or followed another child into a store thinking that maybe it was their own child and there had been a "mix up." Convey an uncritical response to the grieving parent's stories and behavior. Short of committing a crime, almost any reaction of the bereaved is "normal." Parents hang on by a thread.

+ Talk with your friends about their marriage.

Even the most solid marriage can be seriously affected by the death of a child. Don't assume your friends' marriage is holding up perfectly under the pressure. Ask them how they're doing. Ask them if anything has changed between them. Encourage them to open up to one another with their grief, emotions, and perspectives on the death. Many times grieving couples haven't addressed those topics with each other—and the longer they hold it in, the more distant they'll become from one another. You may also want to encourage your friends to see a marriage and/or a grief counselor.

+ Continue to support your friends through the long haul.

Even once your friends seem to be fine, it's important to continue your support. Regularly ask them how they're doing. Talk about the child and the death. Encourage them to continually seek God's comfort during the hard times. Send a card or note every year on the child's birthday to remind the parents that you're still thinking of them and praying for them.

SCRIPTURE HELP

These Scriptures can help you and your friends as you support them through the intense pain of losing a child.

+ Psalm 18:6
+ Psalm 31:9
+ Psalm 147:3
+ Matthew 26:36-38
+ John 13:34-35

+ Romans 8:37-39
+ 2 Corinthians 4:8
+ 2 Corinthians 6:3-10
+ Philippians 1:6
+ 1 Peter 3:8

Group Tips

✛ Be there in the beginning.

Pool your resources as a group to take care of the parents and family immediately following the death.

Have someone either with them or on call at all times—Encourage group members to sign up for certain times of day when they can call or stop by to comfort the family.

Take food—The parents won't be up to the task of cooking. Create a sign up sheet so group members (and other interested people in the church) can sign up to take food every night for at least the first two weeks after the death.

Meet practical needs—Do they need someone to drive their kids to school? to pick up extended family at the airport? to clean their house before or after the funeral? to go grocery shopping for them? to help with funeral arrangements? No detail is too small—your friends will be struggling with even the most basic tasks of everyday life. Be there to help them. Ask what they need.

✛ Be there in the middle.

One of the most common complaints grieving parents have about their church community is that people were there in the beginning but dropped out of sight after a few weeks. Don't let that happen! The most difficult and painful times for grieving parents are in the weeks after the funeral.

Pray—Pray regularly for the family during your small group time, on your own, and with the family. Ask your friends if they have specific prayer requests. You may even want to create a prayer sign-up sheet for your group so you know that the family's requests are being prayed for regularly.

Let the family talk—One mother said, "If you want to clear a room fast, mention your child died!" Encourage a caring and supportive group atmosphere where your grieving friends can express their pain, can talk about their child, and can even state anger at God. Don't judge, preach at, or hush the family show empathy, compassion, and love as you listen to their hurt.

Continue offering help with the practical things—Ask regularly if there's anything the group can do for the family.

Be sure they keep coming—Don't let your friends disappear. Many grieving parents will withdraw from the church or small group. Don't let that happen! Continue pursuing your friends. Invite them to get-togethers, nights out, and other group or family functions.

+ There is no end...just keep being there.

Your friends will always feel pain. The grief of losing a child lasts a lifetime. Never shy away from talking about it with your friends. Never tell them to just move on. Instead, show your continued support through prayer, love, and thoughtful actions. Send cards on important days, such as the child's birthday or the anniversary of his or her death. Let the parents know you're still thinking about them and you'll be there for them if they ever need anything.

ADDITIONAL RESOURCES

+ Books

Klass, Dennis. *The Spiritual Lives of Bereaved Parents.* London: Brunner/Mazel, 1999.

Rando, Therese A. *Parental Loss of a Child.* Champaign, IL: Research Press, 1986.

Jorden, John C. *Spirituality and Loss.* Ashland: Ashland Theological Seminary Press, 2005.

+ Online Resources

www.compassionatefriends.org (The Compassionate Friends)

What Not to Say

+ "God wanted your child with him."

This kind of statement is a perfect example of how, in bad timing, the truth can be offensive. This can make parents feel that God is punishing them or angry with them.

+ "Well, at least you have your other children."

Similar to "You're still young; you can have more kids." Don't tie positive things to sorrow; they're completely unrelated, and one can't diminish the other or replace the emptiness. Recognize your friends' grief; don't try to take it away.

+ "It's a blessing that it happened now instead of later."

Don't try to give hurting people something to feel "grateful" for. Besides, time and age have no effect on the impact this loss has. (Same with: "Oh, it happened a long time ago, you should be over it by now.")

+ "Everything happens for a reason; God will work this out for good."

This will sound like a meaningless and pat reminder—especially when given soon after a death. It's normal to lose trust and to experience violent grief—so to try to prevent your friends' grief process or push them more quickly through what God's doing is unnecessary and can actually be more harmful.

What to Say

+ "I care about you and am praying for you."

People have all kinds of different coping mechanisms, so don't expect people to handle loss one certain way. Give your friends the freedom to cope in their own way without trying to impart spiritual principles (no matter how true!). Let God work, and wait for the right time to give his words of wisdom.

+ "I don't know what to say. But please know that I'm here for you, whatever you need."

It's OK not to know what to say. Just being present means more than anything else. Be available, be a listener, and be a friend.

+ "What do you need today that I can do for you?"

Remember that, for your friends, normal time ceases to exist. Their schedule does not follow yours. So they may welcome a phone call or meal in the middle of the night.

And never assume someone else in the church or small group is taking the lead in the support efforts. Be the first to pursue your friends with tenderness, immediate help, and loving service—a cup of coffee around the clock, money for a tank of gas, an offer to baby-sit.

+ "Tell me about your child."

Sure, you don't want to make your friends cry, but the truth is they're going to cry anyway. What your friends may need is to have someone cry with them—so don't be scared of their tears. Go through it with them, let them stay for a bit in their grief, and don't try to help them move ahead before they're ready.

Say their child's name. If your friends don't want to talk about him or her, they'll let you know. But if they do, it might be one of the most powerful moments you could be a part of.

+ "How is your marriage doing?"

Don't expect your friends to know how to maneuver through marriage after such a massive blow. Ask how they're holding up together, and offer to help.

Parents who've experienced a child's death need emotional and spiritual support more than any words of counsel. Get into the hurt with them—listen, care, pray, and love.

Chapter 2

The Death of a Spouse
Loving People During Their Greatest Loss

with counseling insights from **A. KOSHY MUTHALALY, PH.D.**
+ ministry tips from **LINDA CRAWFORD**

"*It felt like half of me had been torn away, like I had a big open, gaping wound.*"

Nancy was just 30 years old when she died. For five years she had been Charles' wife and a devoted mother to their two small boys, Chad and Brent. She died two days before Charles' birthday, three days before Thanksgiving, and 18 months after she'd been diagnosed with terminal brain cancer.

It'd been a long 18 months. Charles and Nancy, who was six months pregnant, received the bad news right before Easter. The doctors pronounced a death sentence for Nancy, giving her only 24 months to live. Shaken to the core by the news, the couple sought comfort and hope at a local church on Easter Sunday. As they sat in the hard pew with the doctors' words of death still ringing in their ears, they heard a very different message—a message of love and of a promise of eternal life through faith in Jesus. It was a promise they could not live without. Both Charles and Nancy committed their faith and their lives to Jesus that day.

The doctors first tried removing the tumor through surgery. Miraculously, she was out of the hospital in two days, and 10 days later gave birth to Brent. But the cancer grew back. Friends at church prayed for healing, and the doctors tried radiation therapy. But still it grew back. Despite the best efforts of medicine and prayer, in the end it was the treatment for the cancer, rather than the cancer itself, that took her life.

Even though Charles had known for many months Nancy might not live, he was still unable to handle his emotions when she died. After the funeral service, he didn't stay to allow anyone to comfort him; he just got up and left.

"I didn't want to talk to people. I didn't want to listen to people say they were sorry. I didn't want anything to do with anybody; I just wanted to be alone."

Unable to face people or the magnitude of his sorrow, Charles isolated himself at home. He felt like half of everything about his life was gone. Home wasn't home without Nancy. She was no longer there to do what she had always done, to be who she had always been—a wife, mother, and companion. Despite his intense desire to be alone, Charles made some feeble attempts to stay connected to people during the first weeks after Nancy's death.

"I went to church, but I wasn't involved. I felt so alone. I couldn't read or pray; all I could do was weep."

Charles' friends in his small group saw his struggle and weren't about to let him stay isolated during this difficult time. Ann and Roger were instrumental in mobilizing members to provide the family with meals, babysitting, housecleaning, and regular phone calls of encouragement. Others pitched in and helped with the laundry and Christmas shopping. Many offered prayers and comforting words. Paralyzed by grief, Charles needed everything they could give.

But they had to discern how to help because Charles had no ability to ask for what he needed. He couldn't pick up the phone and call for help with the kids or laundry. He couldn't tell anyone that he needed help with his checkbook or with taking out the trash. He would have understood if people had abandoned him to his loneliness and pain. After all, being alone was the only thing he *could* verbalize he really wanted and needed.

"People respected my wishes for time alone, but they never abandoned me. It was the practical things they did to help that ministered to me the most. That and just being there."

When Nancy died, Charles felt the open wound of grief such a loss brings, but his faith in Jesus brought him healing. And the persistent help and encouragement of his friends in his small group helped him learn how to live—and love—again.

"No matter what I faced, I always knew the Lord was with me. That knowledge was affirmed by my small group. The presence of God with me was seen in the way they kept in touch with me, made contact, served me, and made sure I was doing OK. My small group and friends helped draw me back into life. If I hadn't had that group, I don't know what I would have done. I think the whole outcome would have been much different."

WHEN TO REFER

For most people who are grieving, professional counseling can be very helpful. But in some cases—such as those below—it's *necessary* to seek professional help.

+ When the grief never seems to end—If after a normal period of time (which is different for everyone), your friend still seems to be living in the past and holding on to memories in an effort to keep his or her spouse alive, then it's time to seek professional help.

+ When the grief paralyzes the rest of life—If after a period of time, the grief prevents the person from doing what is necessary, such as caring for him or herself, sustaining a job, or taking care of children, it's a clear indication that professional help is needed.

+ When the person becomes depressed—If after a period of time, the person seems to show signs of depression (see *Chapter 3—Depression*), then it may be time to suggest a counselor.

Care and Counseling Tips

THE BASICS

+ Recognize the range of feelings a person goes through when a spouse dies.

Grief is a journey—it's a process that can't be perfectly defined or completely controlled. That being said, there are some commonly acknowledged stages of grief that most people experience—sometimes in this order and sometimes not.

Denial—*"No, this can't be happening to me."*
Anger—*"God, how could you do this to me?"*
Bargaining—*"I'll do anything; just give her back to me."*
Depression—*"What's the use of living without him?"*
Acceptance—*"I know my spouse is gone forever, but I can still live my life."*

+ Understand the journey of grief.

When a person is grieving, it's important to understand that every person grieves differently. Some people will go methodically through the precise stages described above. Others will skip all around or even experience two stages at once.

Seek to understand where your friend is in the process, and then support him or her in that stage. Don't try to force your friend to grieve in a certain way or try to move too quickly from stage to stage. Acknowledge where your friend is, and then come alongside him or her.

Care Tips

+ Be there.

For most grieving spouses, the hardest part is dealing with the absence of their loved ones in the home. The silence is deafening. The bed is empty. The memories are everywhere. Although reflective alone-time is an important part of the grieving process, the loneliness can be overwhelming. Especially in the beginning, be sure to stop by often and to be available by phone whenever your friend needs you. Offer to stay the night occasionally—nighttime can be especially lonely. Getting out of the house is also important, so take your friend out for dinner, to a museum, or on a hike.

Although anyone—and everyone—should be there for a grieving spouse, it's particularly important for men to reach out to men and women to reach out to women.

+ Help the surviving spouse face the everyday realities.

Sometimes it's the most practical things that help. Your friend just lost his or her partner in life—someone whom they've probably come to depend on: for the main source of income, for balancing the checkbook, for taking the kids to school, or even for doing the dishes. Offer your help in those simple areas. Be there when your friend has to deal with insurance companies, investment brokers, and estate managers. Help your friend find a new job if he or she needs to. There are so many little things that change after someone loses a spouse—those changes can be overwhelming to someone who's grieving. Be willing to help in all the ways you can.

+ Listen. Give your friend the opportunity to share his or her feelings.

Don't be afraid to let your friend reminisce about his or her spouse. Telling stories, sharing memories, and looking through photos are cathartic actions, and they're important parts of the grieving process. Remember birthdays, anniversaries, and other important dates. Inquire about the special things they did together regularly, such as evening walks after dinner, Sunday night movies, or morning prayer. Encourage your friend to share what those times meant to him or her. If possible, participate in some of those activities with your friend. Eventually these actions will become less and less necessary as your friend begins to accept the loss and move on with life—but in the beginning they're critical.

+ Pray with and for your friend.

Don't force your friend to pray if he or she isn't ready, but do offer to pray with your friend. Pray short and pointed prayers, keeping the focus on God and on the grieving person.

When you're away from your friend, remember to pray for him or her—especially at night, as that can be the loneliest time for those grieving.

Ask your friend for specific prayer requests. Does he or she need a job? Are his or her kids having a particularly hard time? Is your friend challenged by everyday activities? Finding out specific prayer requests will help you pray for the right things, but it will also help your friend identify where and when he or she is struggling most. Knowing this can help with the grieving process as it directs intentional focus on those areas.

SCRIPTURE HELP

These Scriptures can help you and your friend as you face the pain of loss.

+ **Psalm 34:18**
+ **Psalm 86:1-7**
+ **Psalm 94:18-19**
+ **Psalm 126:4-6**
+ **Isaiah 40:31**

+ **Matthew 5:4**
+ **Romans 8:37-39**
+ **Romans 12:15**
+ **2 Corinthians 1:3-4**
+ **Revelation 7:15-17**

Counseling Tips

There are many ways that you can counsel someone who has just lost a spouse, but it's also important to realize that many grieving spouses will benefit most from working with a trained grief counselor. Use these tips as you personally care for and counsel your friend, but don't be afraid to suggest a professional counselor as well.

✛ Support the person at every stage.

The many stages of grief include—and usually start with—shock or denial. Denial is a normal coping mechanism, and it protects the individual from experiencing too many intense emotions too quickly. If a grieving spouse instantly realized and accepted the full reality of his or her loss, with all of the ramifications, he or she would be overwhelmed. However, by accepting the loss a little at a time, the person can deal with it slowly.

Once your friend begins to *feel* his or her emotions, don't expect him or her to just go through a stage and neatly move on to the next. Expect instead to see your friend cycle through the stages—to experience guilt one day (or even one hour) and then depression the next, then back to guilt again and then on to anger.

You may find it easiest to deal with your friend's sadness and depression because those feelings seem like the most acceptable and expected emotional reactions to loss. However, it's crucial that you allow and encourage your friend to experience and work through *each* of the stages and emotions. Don't discourage your friend from feeling anger—at God, at people, even at the deceased spouse. Don't stop your friend from expressing guilt regarding the death, the relationship, the last words he or she had with the spouse. Each of the emotions is an important and natural part of the grieving process, and it's critical that you support your friend through *all* of the stages—even the ones that may seem negative or counterproductive.

+ Encourage the person to make a scrapbook.

Looking through and sorting old pictures, little notes, audio or video clips, and old cards can all be cathartic in the healing process. They keep memories fresh, of course. But even more importantly, they'll often provoke the grief that's just under the surface. Once that grief has surfaced, the person—with your help and with God's help—can work through that grief. It may seem as if looking at these tokens and exploring the memories is making the grief worse, but in reality it's bringing to the surface what otherwise might fester underneath and never be dealt with.

+ Remember to keep in touch.

Most people have a lot of support during the first few days and weeks after losing a spouse. People come to the funeral; they send flowers and food; they pray for the grieving spouse. But after a few weeks, much of the support stops. But it's during this time that your friend may need support the most. Stop by regularly; send notes; call or e-mail daily; take your friend out to dinner. And be sure that your friend knows that you're *always* available if he or she needs to talk.

ADDITIONAL RESOURCES

+ Books

Baumgardner, Barbara. *A Passage Through Grief: A Recovery Guide.* Nashville, TN: Broadman and Holman Publishers, 2002.

Davis, Verdell. *Let me Grieve, But Not For Ever: A Journey Out of the Darkness and Loss.* Dallas, TX: Word Publishing, 1994.

Lewis, C.S. *A Grief Observed.* San Francisco, CA: HarperCollins, 2001.

+ Online Resources

www.troubledwith.com

Group Tips

When someone in your small group loses a spouse, it's important to remember that it takes the small group by surprise as well. More than likely, many of your small group members just lost a good friend. Everyone in your small group will be going through a grief process. Set up time to talk with all of your small group members to help them through this time—and to give them ideas for helping the surviving spouse. He or she will need to have daily doses of encouragement and support. Your small group will be an essential part of his or her healing process.

+ Support your friend.

The days and months immediately following the funeral are usually the hardest for the bereaved. When family and close friends begin to leave, then the reality of life alone sets in. It's important that the small group keeps in touch during this time so the person gets the support he or she needs. Be sensitive to the fact that the person will need private time. Don't have small group members visiting every hour of every day, but ask plainly what the person needs and when. Then ask people in the small group to volunteer their time and gifts to fulfill those needs.

+ Provide support in the small group.

As depression sets in, your friend may lose the desire to attend church or small group meetings. Don't let your friend become disconnected! Even if he or she doesn't want to come to the meetings, organize times when the whole group can go out together or visit the bereaved. It's important that he or she stay connected and social—whether the person wants to or not!

+ Meet specific immediate needs.

Sometimes the seemingly trivial things are the most important. During the grief process, the many small details can become overwhelming. In your small group, you may have lawyers, financial specialists, mechanics, cooks, and other experts. Pool the expertise from your small group to help with immediate needs, such as the execution of the will, understanding financial obligations, arranging the funeral service, cooking food, doing laundry, taking care of children, finding a job if needed...and so on. Help with all those little things will really add up to a huge blessing for your friend!

+ Coordinate your group's efforts.

It's important at times of bereavement that the small group elects a coordinator who can organize the helping efforts. Bereavement in many ways can be considered a crisis, and it calls for crisis management. Your coordinator should make sure that helping efforts are not duplicated and that specific needs are being met.

+ Remember long term needs.

Just because the grieving spouse seems to be doing OK and carrying on as normal, it doesn't mean that he or she is set for life. There are many things your small group can continue to do as your friend works through the grieving process. Send a card on, or acknowledge in other ways, the birthday, marriage anniversary, and death anniversary of the deceased, as well as other times that might be particularly difficult, such as holidays. Talk with the surviving spouse about what it means to be single and alone again. Invite your friend to the occasional night out, party, or special event. And always be ready and willing to listen when he or she is going through a hard time.

What Not to Say

+ "Your spouse is in heaven."

Even if this is true, it doesn't minimize the loss that the surviving spouse is going through. The grief and loss he or she is facing are very real, tangible things. The loss of a life partner is significant, and to undermine that is to be insensitive to the bereaved person's pain.

+ "Maybe we should have prayed harder."

People often try to find an explanation for why someone died. Unfortunately, what these problem-solving types of statements really convey to the grieving spouse is a sense of guilt. Avoid any "if only," "we should have," or "maybe if" statements—these sound like a blame game, and the grieving spouse is the one who will feel most responsible for the death.

+ "Don't worry, God has a new mate for you."

This statement invalidates the need to mourn the loss of a loved one, and implies the person should find comfort in hoping for a replacement spouse. Remember, your friend already committed to a lifetime of love and companionship with his or her spouse, and that love deserves honor and respect. This comment subtly implies that his or her spouse was just a light bulb and God is going to help change it.

What to Say

+ "I'm so sorry; this is a terrible loss."

The most powerful words of comfort can be conveyed by sharing in and validating the person's grief. There are no better words to say, especially when you don't know what to say, than, "I'm so sorry."

+ "I'm here for you. Can I call you in a few days?"

Many people will say, "I'm here for you, call me if you need anything" to a grieving spouse. Better to ask if you can call and then commit to doing so. It's important to realize that most people who are mourning are not able to reach out and ask for help. The person will need you to take the responsibility for contact. But don't offer to "be there" if you don't mean to follow through. Be a visible presence, not an invisible promise.

+ "As your friends, we're going to help you through this. You're not alone."

These words can be a source of encouragement, and they let the person know that he or she has friends who can be counted on when times get tough. Caring small group members can help alleviate the fear and uncertainty your friend is feeling.

+ "Please let us know what your specific needs are so we can help you."

We don't always know what the specific needs are during a time of crisis and bereavement. So it's perfectly OK to ask! If your friend isn't ready with an answer, ask what specific prayer requests he or she has.

Chapter 3

Depression

Supporting Your Friend in the Darkness

with counseling insights from
REBEKAH KNIGHT-BAUGHMAN, PH.D.
+ ministry tips from AMY WEAVER

I've always had a personality susceptible to depression. Depression isn't a sign of personal weakness or a condition that can be willed or wished away, despite what many people think. People like me who struggle with depression can't simply "pull themselves" together and get better.

The first time I experienced a deep depression, I felt lost. I was dealing with issues I'd never dealt with before. I'd essentially lost my dad through a divorce, and the feelings surrounding that experience created the depression that plagued me. Those feelings of being lost and alone were compounded when I lost the support of my mother and sister—I moved across the country to go to college, and I became a Christian—two things they really didn't like. I felt abandoned when I needed support the most.

It was during that first year of college when I realized I had a serious problem. That was when I started failing...for the first time in my life. I'd always been successful in everything I did—I was an A student in school, a star on the track team, the editor of my school yearbook. But I just couldn't make myself do any of it anymore, and it wasn't long before I was on academic probation. Sure, I was discouraged about school, but it wasn't enough to get me out of the slump I'd sunk into. Eventually, I just stopped going to classes. Everything seemed like too much work.

My sophomore year of college, I promised myself I'd do better in school. But before the semester even began, I felt those familiar thoughts creeping in. I was overwhelmed before I even started. I felt unworthy of another chance, unworthy of love. I felt sorry for myself, like things were unfair and like nobody around me understood how I felt. I needed to know I was loved, so I tried to draw attention to myself. I tried to be funny, spiritual, encouraging—anything to get people to acknowledge me. It didn't last long—the effort was too much. So in the end, I just started avoiding people.

During this time, I didn't sleep or eat for days. And then at other times, I slept or ate way too much. I was a case of extremes. I cried a lot and then felt numb. I didn't want to bathe or get out of bed for days on end. I wrote in my journal that I wanted to be alone because no one understood me or knew what I needed. People felt fake. I wanted it all to go away. I felt helpless and hopeless.

For the most part, people in my small group didn't have a clue about what I was going through, and that hurt. Some people tried to fix me. When I didn't get better immediately they either got frustrated with me or gave up on me. They told me I wasn't seeking God or I needed to try harder to get over my depression—as if all it would take was a simple "attitude adjustment."

But that wasn't everyone. There were those who were there for me. They listened to what I had to say. They sincerely cared about understanding what I was going through. They didn't simply offer quick fixes; instead they prayed for me and with me. They encouraged me by speaking truth into my life, writing notes, showing me how important I was to them. Those unexpected gestures were done out of love, and they meant the world to me.

They pursued me when I thought I wanted to be alone. Getting out of my room and out of my bed was a positive thing, even if only to help me focus on something besides myself. When I said "no" to going places, they gently insisted. They told me they wanted me with them and expressed that I was important to them with their words and actions. It was what I needed.

And, really, it was those little things that got me out of the depression: prayer, love, meaningful actions, simple activities, a gift for no reason, an offer to watch my favorite movie, a listening ear, a special dinner made for me by special friends. God's love offered to me through God's people. They reminded me that God still loved me even if I didn't see him.

God worked through the people in my small group, and I gradually began to come out of my depression. It took time and effort on the part of the people around me. I started to take part in all the daily activities that I'd been avoiding, and my mood improved little by little. Some days were harder than others. And though I'll most likely always be susceptible to depression, I know that I have friends who will help me through it.

ADDITIONAL RESOURCES

+ Books

Tan, Siang-Yang and Ortberg, John. *Coping with Depression.* Grand Rapids, MI: Baker Books, 2004.

Worthington, Everett, L., Jr. *When Someone Asks for Help: A Practical Guide for Counseling.* Downers Grove, IL: InterVarsity Press, 1982.

+ Online Resources

www.nimh.nih.gov/publicat/friend.cfm
(National Institute of Mental Health)

www.healthyminds.org (American Psychiatric Association)

www.suicidology.org (American Association of Suicidology)

www.dbsalliance.org (Depression and Bipolar Support Alliance)

Care and Counseling Tips

THE BASICS

Depression is a dark and oppressive mood problem that can feel unbearable to the person suffering from it. The burden of depression drags the person down as he or she tries to carry on with life as usual when life is not "as usual." Yet there is hope. By understanding the basic symptoms and causes for depression and learning to express care in ways that will be received well by the person who is depressed, you can share the burden of depression with your friend, and he or she will begin to feel the weight of depression lift. Look for the following symptoms if you think a group member may be depressed.

+ Emotional Symptoms of Depression

A depressed mood is usually characterized by hopelessness, sadness, discouragement, anxiety, and/or irritability all day, nearly every day for two weeks. These internal feelings may manifest in behaviors such as frequent crying, sharp and hurtful comments, a pessimistic outlook, and statements that reveal a sense of being overwhelmed by life.

+ Physical Symptoms of Depression

The body has a way of manifesting symptoms when a person is suffering emotionally. Depressed people may experience a change in appetite and in sleep patterns. In addition, depressed people tend to have several physical complaints and often take more trips to the doctor than usual.

+ Cognitive Symptoms of Depression

People who experience depression tend to think negatively about themselves. You may notice your friend making self-deprecating comments such as, "You're a great leader. I could never lead without messing the whole thing up." Moreover, the person may have difficulty thinking clearly, concentrating, or making decisions. If untreated, depression can lead to thoughts of death or, in the worst case, suicide. Be sensitive to comments such as, "I just want to fall asleep forever" or "I can't go on like this anymore."

+ Behavioral Symptoms of Depression

Decreased energy, tiredness, and fatigue are characteristics of depression. You may notice that your friend's house has not been cleaned in some time, personal hygiene has declined, he or she is sleeping much more than usual, and your friend isn't enjoying things he or she normally loves.

+ Spiritual Symptoms of Depression

When a person is depressed, he or she may have a hard time connecting with God and believing in God's goodness and providence. Prayer may become difficult for the person, as he or she may feel hopeless or guilty for not praying enough, in the right way, or about the right things. If the person's individual spirituality suffers during depression, corporate spirituality is likely to suffer as well. That is, he or she may have difficulty getting to church due to fatigue, and once at church worship may be difficult.

+ Reasons for Depression

Most mental health practitioners agree that the combination of internal and external factors affect a person's mood. Here are some common influencers of depression:

• Genetic, biochemical, and hormonal factors
• Family history of depression
• Loss within relationship—death, divorce, or geographical relocation
• Feeling unsafe and insecure in relationships
• Change in employment status
• Dissatisfaction in work and/or work environment
• Negative thinking

Care Tips

When a person is experiencing depression, it's difficult to know how to be present with him or her in the darkness. You want to let your friend know that you are caring and supportive, but you may feel drained by the heaviness and pessimism when you are with the person. Here are some tips to help you serve your friend in the struggle to get out of depression.

+ Actively listen.

Encouraging your friend to talk about his or her sadness will foster understanding, which can help the person feel a sense of control over emotions instead of feeling controlled by emotions. Although the feelings may frighten you, don't be afraid; just listen as you would to any friend of yours.

+ Spend time with your friend.

When a person is depressed, the natural tendency is to hide from others and try to recover on one's own. Your friend may be hiding because he or she is afraid of appearing weak or disturbed. But that's exactly the opposite of what is needed. A depressed person needs other people! Your presence will help shoulder the burden of depression, allow for rest, stave off loneliness, guard against suicide, and provide strength.

+ Suggest enjoyable activities.

Your depressed friend may not be able to come up with enjoyable activities due to a lack of excitement and joy. So share your joy! Suggest activities that he or she once enjoyed or those that you enjoy. Even if your friend seems resistant, there is a part of him or her that longs to do enjoyable things—it's simply buried under depression. Be persistent—human contact and enjoyable activities are good for the person!

+ Exercise.

It's a vicious cycle. The fatigue and lack of motivation caused by depression significantly impairs a depressed person's ability to exercise...but regular exercise has been shown to be a buffer against depression. You will be helping your friend immensely by committing to regular exercise with him or her. Do it once a week, twice a week, or even once a day—any little bit will help! Play a sport, take an exercise class, or walk together after dinner.

+ Prepare meals.

When a friend is depressed, he or she may lose the motivation to cook and the desire to eat. Offer to prepare meals for your friend or to cook together. The food and the fellowship will be invaluable!

+ Be nonjudgmental.

Depressed people judge themselves every day, so the last thing they need is a friend who judges them, too. Communicate patience and grace. By doing this, you may help your friend become more patient and gracious toward him or herself.

SCRIPTURE HELP

These Scriptures can help you and your friend as you face the depression together.

+ **Psalms 31; 32:1-7**
+ **Psalm 42:1-5**
+ **Psalm 139**
+ **Isaiah 40:29-31**
+ **Jeremiah 17:5-8**

+ **Romans 15:13**
+ **2 Corinthians 1:3-11**
+ **2 Corinthians 4:8-9**
+ **Ephesians 6:10-18**
+ **Philippians 4:4-8**

Counseling Tips

Many times depression calls for a professional counselor. Even so, there are many ways you can personally help counsel your friend through this tough time.

+ Build and maintain trust.
Trust takes time—it takes positive experiences built on more positive experiences. But once trust is built, it's easy to break—especially when things said in secret are later shared with others. As you counsel your friend, be sure to keep a policy of confidentiality—the *only* time you should talk to someone else without your friend's permission is if your friend is abusing him or herself or another person.

+ Validate and normalize emotions.
Without crawling into the pit of depression with your friend, you can validate his or her emotions by expressing understanding and care. Normalizing depression can also help the person feel less alone in the process. By recalling another friend or family member who struggles with mood problems, you may bring the depressed person a sense of relief that he or she is not the first or the last person to go through such a struggle.

+ Challenge faulty thinking.
Depression impairs people's thinking. Depressed people often feel unworthy of good relationships, success on the job, or a peaceful lifestyle. They often think that God has cursed them and that life is hopeless. If your friend expresses these feelings, gently challenge him or her, and speak the truth of God's love for him or her. Remind your friend that recovery from depression is a process, but it's treatable through professional counseling, fellowship, prayer, time, and medication if necessary.

+ Create positive affirmations.

Depression clouds the ability to think positively. One way to counter this is to help your friend come up with positive affirmations about him or herself. For instance, he or she may state, "I am treasured by God and worthy of love" or "I am a good artist." It doesn't matter if your friend wholeheartedly believes the affirmation or not, it will still serve as a reminder of who one is—a beloved creation and child of God. Encourage your friend to repeat the affirmations daily.

+ Trust God for your friend.

Don't be afraid to make mistakes! Trust God as you learn to care for and counsel your friend. Pray for your friend regularly, and ask God to give you wisdom and insight into your friend's heart.

WHEN TO REFER

+ When your friend becomes suicidal—If your friend expresses a desire to end his or her life, get help. (Refer to *Chapter 4—Suicide* for more guidelines.)

+ When your friend is a danger to others—If your friend expresses a sincere desire to harm another person, refer him or her to a mental healthcare worker, and notify the person whom he or she has plans to harm.

+ When a child is endangered or neglected—If your friend has children or works with children and he or she is unable to care for them, encourage the person to get help, offer to take the children for a time if you're able, or notify child protective services.

+ When your friend's daily functioning is impaired—Depression can impair a person's social, occupational, and personal functioning. If you know that the person is not engaging socially, their work performance is suffering, or your friend is unable to get out of bed, eat, groom, and/or bathe, get help.

Group Tips

A small group can be a *huge* source of support and strength to a friend struggling with depression. These tips will help your group minister to your friend.

✛ Talk about it.

Every person in a group influences every other person in the group. Together, identify ways in which the depression has influenced the group. Some people may notice that they're feeling depressed, frustrated, compassionate, or even angry. Take time to help people understand and empathize with the depressed person. As a group, talk about and research the dynamics of depression. Ask your depressed friend to share how he or she is feeling. Encourage others to share their own experiences with depression. Promote compassion, empathy, and knowledge within your group.

✛ Pray together.

Prayer can be one of the most important factors in fighting depression. Encourage your friend to share specific prayer requests during the group time. Pray together as a group, and also ask group members to pray daily for their friend.

✛ Show your support in fun, practical ways.

Create care baskets—Include cards, encouraging Scripture verses, herbal tea, music, movies, energy bars, gift certificates, and other fun things!

Regularly have group fun nights—Tailor them to your friend's liking by doing the things you know he or she used to enjoy.

Check in on the person—Organize a visit and phone call list that covers the person for a month at a time. Be sure that someone is either calling or visiting that person every day—especially in the early part of the depression. Once your friend has found a counselor and stabilized emotionally, the frequency of visits and phone calls could decrease to once per week.

Affirm your friend—Regularly send encouraging notes, "out of the blue" gifts, and funny e-mails. These will serve as reminders of your love and support.

+ Remember...

Reaching out to a person who is swimming in sadness and hopelessness is the best thing you can do! Don't give up—your efforts are making a huge difference.

HELPING A FRIEND FIND HELP

+ Assess your friend's openness—You need to establish where your friend falls in terms of his or her openness to seeking help from a professional.

+ Deal with resistance—If your friend resists the idea of seeking help, ask why. Point out that people who have physical pain see a doctor. It's as natural for people with emotional pain to seek professional help.

+ Educate—Together, research what counseling is all about.

+ Follow up—As your friend ventures into counseling in order to manage depression, he or she will likely appreciate your continued support—ask general questions, pray for your friend, and affirm him or her regularly.

What Not to Say

+ "As Christians, we should show the joy of the Lord."

This statement leaves no room for the spectrum of emotions common to the human experience. By making statements like this, you'll only cause your friend to feel further away from God than he or she already does. Your friend is probably aware that depression is not God's emotional design for anyone, and yet he or she still can't stop being depressed. As Christians, we should be human and show support and love when our brothers or sisters are struggling to find joy.

+ "Stop being so negative, and look at the positive."

This statement may be said with good intentions, but looking at the good things in life isn't the answer for a person with serious depression. While negative thought patterns are one aspect of depression, it's a more complicated matter—depression isn't a choice and can't just disappear with an attitude adjustment. If your friend could simply "not be so negative," he or she would. Saying something of this nature would be like telling a blind person to not be so blind.

+ "I know that you're better than this—don't give in!"

Saying this suggests that your friend is falling short and somehow failing to control his or her emotions. Your friend is likely already dealing with issues of self-worth and feelings of failure—this statement will only confirm those feelings.

What to Say

+ "God is with you in this dark time."

By telling your friend this, you're reminding him or her of the relentless presence of God in all emotional states. You're telling the person that

God is no stranger to depression and he won't leave or disappear when life is tough.

+ "How can I pray for you?"

In this statement, you're communicating that you wish to accommodate your friend spiritually as he or she journeys through this darkness.

+ "I love you."

Although this may seem too simple, when it's said often enough and demonstrated, it can make all the difference.

+ "If you ever need anything, I'm here. I'll call you on Friday to see how you're doing."

Someone struggling with depression has a hard time taking a first step with friends and needs to be pursued. Letting someone know you'll be there can be powerful. Be sincere, and then follow through on your words.

+ "I've been thinking about you today."

This statement reveals that you care. Follow it with thoughtful questions. Anything that shows you listened to a previous conversation and remembered what your friend said will demonstrate that you believe he or she is worth listening to and paying attention to.

+ "You're doing a great job with..."

Again, you're confirming that the person with depression is worthwhile, despite what he or she may be feeling. You're focusing on positive things even if he or she is incapable of doing so.

FINDING A COUNSELOR

Below are some things to consider when looking for a therapist.

+ Gender—Most people will know whether they want a male or female counselor. Be sure to ask your friend this, and help to find a counselor of that gender.

+ Fee—If your friend has financial constraints, he or she may need to find a counselor who works on a sliding scale. This means the counselor will charge a fee based on the person's income. Your friend may wish to utilize any mental health benefits provided by insurance. Community mental health centers tend to charge very little in comparison to private practitioners. However, these centers are designed to serve the masses, including persons with severe mental illnesses. Your friend would need to feel comfortable with that setting.

+ Theoretical orientation—Counselors vary in their approach to working with clients. Counselors can focus on any of the following: (a) changing maladaptive thoughts and behaviors, (b) looking at the family of origin and developing healthy relationships, (c) providing support and unconditional positive regard, (d) making meaning out of life and problems, or (e) a combination of methods. You may help your friend determine one goal for treatment and seek a counselor whose approach can help him or her reach that goal.

+ Spirituality—For some people spirituality is an important component to the therapeutic relationship. A Christian person who struggles with depression may desire a Christian counselor so that the beliefs inherent to the faith can be used in healing.

+ Education and training—Counselor education and training can be just as varied as theoretical orientation. *Biblical counselors* are typically lay leaders who have biblical knowledge and gifts of mercy and exhortation. *Masters-level counselors* have spent two to three years in a graduate program for counseling or clinical psychology. *Clinical psychologists* have five to seven years of graduate schooling and can perform psychological testing and diagnosis of problems. *Psychiatrists* have gone to medical school and are able to prescribe medication.

Chapter 4

Suicide
Intervening Before It's Too Late

with counseling insights **+** ministry tips from
KELLY M. FLANAGAN, PH.D. **+**
KELLY SCHIMMEL FLANAGAN, PH.D.

Emergency Response Handbook: *Susan, thank you for taking the time to meet with us today and for trusting us with such a vulnerable area of your life.*

Susan: I'm happy to help. Suicide is something that doesn't get talked about very much, and we need to open up the subject—especially within the church, which is supposed to be a place of safe harbor for hurting people.

ERH: *Can you identify the first time you seriously thought about suicide?*

Susan: Definitely. I'd been depressed since I was a kid, but I'd never really done anything about it. All three of my sons have struggled with ADHD (attention-deficit hyperactivity disorder) and depression (they often go hand-in-hand), and we finally took my youngest son to the counselor at our church. The counselor actually recognized the symptoms of depression in me, and I began individual counseling. In a way it was helpful because it was the first time I had ever gotten a chance to focus on myself. Anyway, self-awareness is one thing, but change is something else. And my depression was just getting worse—especially as my marriage started to crumble. I started antidepressant medication, but that just made it worse because I felt like a failure for having to try it. Finally my marital problems became so intense that I told my counselor during a session that I was thinking of hurting myself. He did the right thing and escorted me to a nearby emergency room, where they admitted me to the psychiatric ward.

ERH: *Prior to your hospitalization, was your church or small group a source of support?*

Susan: The church was a source of support in the sense that it gave me a place to which I could escape. I felt useful there: I was a Sunday school teacher, a member of the executive board, and a small group leader. I also joined another small group focused on specific spiritual gifts. In that group I felt accepted and affirmed, which was a new experience for me.

ERH: *While in the hospital, was the church or small group supportive?*

Susan: Yes, during my first hospitalization, I felt incredibly supported by the church and my small group. The pastor's wife visited me several times. She was very kind and made a real effort to cheer me up. A good friend from my small group also visited me every day. She made me laugh a lot during a difficult time...I'm not sure what I would have done without her.

ERH: *What happened the second time?*

Susan: I was hospitalized again almost exactly a year later. I had been working really hard to not appear depressed, and I must have been successful. Then in small group one Sunday, I was giving a brief presentation on a book I had read, and I listed the warning signs of depression and suicidal thoughts. I think it was a cry for help because the more quickly you intervene with someone, the more manageable the problem is. It's a lot easier to stop someone at the top of a hill than halfway down after picking up momentum. That Sunday I even told the group I was really struggling, but no one said anything—they just couldn't believe I was feeling that way. Later that week, I took enough medication to put me to sleep for a long time. I woke up to a friend's phone call. She noticed my grogginess, and when I couldn't promise her I wouldn't take more medication, she picked me up and took me to the hospital. It was demoralizing—I thought I had beat it the first time.

ERH: *When you returned to church the second time, did you feel supported or not?*

Susan: A little bit of both, actually. The pastor's wife thought I was being manipulative. We'd had a dispute earlier in the month, and she thought I was punishing her. Ironically, the dispute was because she thought someone as "unstable" as me was not qualified to serve in leadership positions. She was mad at me, but there was nothing I could do.

The good friend from my small group was very accepting, and she called to check up on me on a daily basis. That felt really good. But I think the fact that I actually took a step toward killing myself really scared off a lot of people. It's funny, or maybe a little sad, that more people felt comfortable talking about the sinfulness of my divorce than they did talking about suicide. Most people just continued to ignore it.

ERH: *Did you prefer that to getting a lot of attention?*

Susan: I felt if I had been in the hospital for a cancer relapse or some other serious physical illness, I would have gotten a lot of support. People would have visited, sent cards and flowers, brought dinners for my kids. But there was none of that. Too much attention may have been uncomfortable, but I think the quiet acts of support would have been a nice middle ground.

ERH: *At the time, you were in a mental health group and also a small group at your church. How did your mental health group handle your relapse compared to your small group?*

Susan: The people in the mental health group were very supportive because they expected you to have these issues and they wanted to communicate about them. On the other hand, I think it takes a lot of work to understand suicide if you haven't been through it, and I think people were either too scared, too judgmental, or too lazy to try. I think most people are scared to death (ha, sorry for the pun) to even address the issue.

ERH: *Ultimately, what would have been most helpful to you?*

Susan: I think it would have been most helpful for people to make themselves available. People who are depressed tend to isolate, which makes it worse. I asked certain friends to call me on certain days of the week. Many of them didn't, and that was pretty painful. But some did, and it was a huge source of support—especially when they asked me to do something with them, such as joining them on a family outing and insisting that I go, even when I initially resisted due to my depression. A lot of days, it was probably the difference between life and death.

Care and Counseling Tips

THE BASICS

As a small group leader, you're unlikely to face anything that frightens you as much as a small group member who is considering suicide. Ultimately, your job is simple—to persuade the person to get professional help. However, reality is often more complex. The first thing to do is learn to detect the presence of suicidal thoughts. Many people will directly tell you that they're thinking about suicide. For others, you'll have to know the warning signs, which fall into two categories: what the person says and what the person does.

+ What the Person Says

People experiencing this kind of emotional pain may communicate it verbally, although perhaps in a disguised way. Types of verbal warnings may include any of the following:

1. Any comment that implies life isn't worth the effort. For instance, "Life's too painful; I don't think I want to deal with it anymore."

2. Any comment that shows the person believes there's no solution to his or her problems. For example, "There's no way out of this mess."

3. Any statement implying that others "would be better off" if the person wasn't around.

4. An offer to give up some essential possessions because they'll no longer be needed. For example, "You can have some of my clothes; I don't think I'll be needing them."

5. Any indication that the person may take revenge by hurting him or herself. For instance, "She'll wish she hadn't said that when I'm gone."

+ What the Person Does

Sometimes a suicide attempt is impulsive, but sometimes it isn't, and the person begins to plan for it. The person may begin to make financial arrangements for family, give away personal items or more money than usual, or plan a suicide note. People may also begin to engage in reckless and dangerous activities, such as increasing alcohol and drug use. Other signs include dramatic mood changes, intense anxiety, or signs of depression (see *Chapter 3—Depression*). Most importantly, if the person has begun to develop a plan (if he or she has bought a weapon, stored up pills, or thought about a specific scenario such as jumping off a nearby bridge), he or she is at *high* risk for suicide.

—*Some information in this section is adapted from www.stopasuicide.org.*

ADDITIONAL RESOURCES

+ Books

Fine, Carla. *No Time to Say Goodbye: Surviving the Suicide of A Loved One.* New York, NY: Broadway Books, 1997.

+ Online Resources

www.stopasuicide.org (Screening for Mental Health, Inc.)

www.suicidology.org (American Association of Suicidology)

www.afsp.org/index-1.htm (American Foundation for Suicide Prevention)

www.spanusa.org (Suicide Prevention Action Network USA)

Care Tips

If your friend has told you directly that he or she is considering suicide or you have detected one or more of the warning signs, it is now *essential* that you ACT quickly and lovingly. (ACT is a useful acronym for remembering your responsibilities. See www.stopasuicide.org for more information.) The following are guidelines for your immediate response.

✛ Acknowledge the problem.

Take it seriously—Never doubt your friend is actually considering suicide.

Listen without judgment or criticism—This will increase your credibility when you suggest professional help, and it may increase your friend's willingness to agree.

✛ Care for your friend.

Voice your concern—Ask what is troubling your friend. Be gentle, and try to overcome your friend's reluctance to open up about his or her thoughts.

Express care and understanding—Assure your friend that he or she will be supported in this crisis. Assure the person that, though a real feeling, it's also temporary and that the usual cause of suicidal thoughts, depression, can be treated. (Also refer to *Chapter 3—Depression.*)

Find out if your friend has a specific plan—How detailed is the plan? Has he or she taken any steps toward implementing the plan? Has a time and a place been set? Encourage your friend to talk about his or her plans, and determine the seriousness of the threat.

✛ Treatment—always get help immediately.

If your friend is willing to accept help—Take him or her to the local emergency room or mental health center. You can also contact your friend's primary care physician or a mental health provider. Whomever you choose to contact, stay with your friend, and accompany him or her to the professional service provider.

If your friend is unwilling to seek help—Call the national help line or your local emergency room for assistance (see the "When to Refer" box below).

WHEN TO REFER

+ Always!—It's always possible that you've overestimated the person's risk of suicide. However, in this situation, it's better to err on the safe side. You'll rest easier knowing that you've done the best thing possible for the person.

+ Always!—If the risk for suicide seems to be high, there are several things you can do. First, your friend could call the National Suicide Prevention Lifeline (1-800-273-TALK). Second, if your friend is unwilling to talk to someone about his or her feelings and plans, you can call 911 for an emergency response team. Finally, you may be of greatest service by driving the person to the nearest emergency room for evaluation.

+ Always!—Even if your friend appears to be at low risk for suicide, you should insist on joining him or her in the process of seeking professional intervention. Professionals include psychologists and counselors, suicide prevention centers, a family doctor, and even your minister. Go with the hurting person to the professional.

Counseling Tips

By now you have helped your friend identify and engage in professional help. Now your job is to support the professional services your friend is receiving and help your friend achieve his or her therapeutic goals. Your contributions may include any of the following:

+ Openly communicate about your friend's suicidal feelings.

Meet the person's need to talk about these feelings with someone besides a counselor. Help your friend develop a sense that others care and want to openly discuss his or her difficulties.

+ Relieve isolation.

Isolation can intensify suicidal thoughts and depression. Consider it your and the small group's job to provide your friend with social support and activities. However, be sensitive to individual preferences in activities, and do not be overbearing. At the same time, don't allow your friend to withdraw from social life and caring friends. Perhaps the best measure of how socially connected the person should be is how much he or she has been socially involved during the happiest periods of his or her life. If your friend would normally seek social contact on a daily basis, try to provide this in a way that is not perceived as overbearing. If your friend tends to connect with your small group only on Wednesday nights and Sunday mornings, try to re-establish this pattern while communicating your willingness to be available more frequently if desired.

+ Remove lethal weapons.

One of the first therapeutic goals of the professional counselor will be to remove all lethal weapons (including things such as pills, guns, knives, and so on) from the person's possession in order to protect the person from impulsively attempting suicide. Make yourself available to complete this task with your friend, and hold him or her accountable for keeping lethal objects out of the home. Each individual will require different levels of accountability. For some individuals, a daily or weekly phone call may be enough. For others, you may need to inspect the home frequently. Try to gauge the honesty of your friend's self-report, and if you have some doubt about his or her safety, ask gently if you might be able to more closely monitor your friend's home and behaviors.

+ Be a safe receptacle of your friend's anger and frustration.

Oftentimes, suicide is preceded by a sense that there is no escape from emotional pain. If you feel up to the challenge, allow your friend to express his or her anger and frustration to you. Help your friend understand the importance of doing so rather than turning those feelings inward and hurting him or herself.

SCRIPTURE HELP

These Scriptures can help you and your friend as you face the realities of suicide together.

+ **Psalm 25:4-7, 15-21**
+ **Isaiah 40:27-31**
+ **Isaiah 41:9-10**
+ **Matthew 10:29-31**
+ **Matthew 11:28-30**

+ **Romans 8:35-39**
+ **2 Corinthians 1:3-11**
+ **2 Corinthians 12:7-10**
+ **Philippians 1:19-26**
+ **1 Peter 5:6-10**

Group Tips

Your small group will be an important part of your friend's recovery process. Your group members can use these tips as they support their hurting friend.

+ Don't dance around the issue.
The person with suicidal intentions likely already feels isolated. The person will feel more so if his or her closest companions don't feel comfortable openly discussing the issue. Communicate a willingness to discuss the issue as you would anything else a small group member struggles with.

+ Get involved in your friend's life. Be a community.
Show interest in the person. Continue to provide a community that he or she can turn to when doubts and emotional pain creep in. Through your involvement, even more than your words, you'll communicate that your friend is valued and worthy. For example, ask your friend if you can meet each Wednesday morning for a Bible study at a local coffee shop. Or call your friend on a weekly basis to invite him or her to lunch. As a small group, plan activities that your friend will enjoy. If the person feels secure with you in these activities, he or she is more likely to disclose to you when suicidal thoughts return. This may do more than anything else to prevent a suicide attempt.

+ Be available to listen; be accepting and nonjudgmental.
As you listen openly to your friend's experience and get involved in the person's life, you'll do more damage than good if you communicate a sense of rejection and judgment. Express your compassion for the person, and model God's grace.

+ Don't offer glib reassurance. Acknowledge the difficulty of the feelings and the need for help.
It can be demoralizing for someone who's considering suicide to be offered glib reassurance. Likely, your friend will have already tried many coping

strategies and may have arrived at the conclusion that recovery is going to be difficult and painful—if not impossible. Try not to invalidate your friend by minimizing the magnitude of the problem.

+ Pray.

In the person's current emotional state, he or she may have difficulty perceiving God as loving and benevolent. You may need to model God's love for your friend until he or she is able to connect with God again. Furthermore, if the person is unable to connect lovingly with God, group prayer will be an important and supportive way of manifesting God's love to your friend.

WHEN A GROUP MEMBER COMMITS SUICIDE

Sometimes, despite everyone's prayers, support, and love, the worst happens: Someone in your group commits suicide. How you respond to the tragedy is critical for your group.

+ Don't let guilt destroy you—You may question everything you said, you may doubt everything you did, you may feel that you should have done more. Don't blame yourself for the person's death. Don't let guilt stop you from supporting the people in your group. Do seek a professional counselor if you feel that would help you in the grieving process.

+ Grieve with your group—Your group of friends will probably go through the stages of grief (see *Chapter 2—The Death of a Spouse*). Each member will travel through the stages at a different pace and in a different order. Talk together regularly, cry together, reminisce together. It might even be beneficial to ask a professional grief counselor to attend your group gathering once or twice.

+ Meet individually with grieving group members—Offer to meet individually with the members of your group to talk through the fears, pain, anger, and other emotions that the suicide may have caused. Watch for signs of depression in any members, and refer people to a professional counselor if you feel it's necessary.

+ Offer practical help to the grieving family—See *Chapter 1—The Death of a Child*, and *Chapter 2—The Death of a Spouse* for practical ways you and your group can help the grieving family.

What Not to Say

+ "I dare you to do it."

Don't laugh—this happens, and people who say it are usually well-intentioned. People think that they'll call the person's bluff by essentially telling him or her to do it. This is a *bad* idea. In the person's hopeless state of mind, it may be further evidence that he or she isn't valued.

+ "Ohmigosh, I can't believe you would even think that!"

Don't act surprised. This response may further the person's sense of shame and guilt, and it won't allow your friend to trust you and your desire to help. The person's problem is very real and very serious—try not to invalidate it.

+ "Sure, I promise not to tell anyone."

Don't let yourself be sworn to secrecy. Also, don't worry if you have already agreed to secrecy. Let your friend know why you won't be able to keep the agreement—he or she may initially be upset, but will thank you in the long run. Feel confident that it's in your friend's best interest to speak with others.

+ "Suicide is a sin."

The last thing the hurting person needs is an intellectual or theological debate. Instead, your friend is probably craving someone who can be there for him or her emotionally. You can be far more helpful if you work hard to empathize with your friend and convince him or her to seek professional help.

+ "Where is your faith? Things will get better."

It *is* important to tell the hurting person that the suicidal feelings are not permanent and that his or her ability to consider alternative solutions will return. However, it's also important to do so *without* questioning the person's faith. As you come alongside your friend and offer care during this trial, you'll naturally have opportunities to increase his or her faith. But to question your friend's faith at the outset will likely put distance between the two of you and decrease your ability to help him or her.

What to Say

+ "Are you thinking about committing suicide?"

Many people hesitate to ask this question due to concern that it will offend the person or will plant the idea in his or her mind. Don't worry about that! With this question, you're more likely to communicate genuine concern than to make someone angry or offended. Furthermore, it's unlikely someone who isn't considering suicide will begin to do so simply because you asked a question.

+ "Let *us* be hopeful for you until you're ready to be hopeful again."

This implies several important things. First, it communicates that everyone is going to be there to support the person. Second, it says that you understand how hopeless your friend feels right now. Third, it communicates that you're confident your friend will emerge from this and be hopeful again.

+ "I know this is an issue that doesn't get talked about enough in the church. When you feel ready, would you be willing to work with me to start a support group for people feeling depressed and suicidal?"

It's very important to communicate that the person is not alone. By saying this, you imply that your friend isn't alone and that people need to be supportively discussing the topic more often in the church. And hope that the person could contribute to helping others is likely to increase his or her sense of self-worth.

+ "I love you, and as your friend in Christ, I won't abandon you during this difficult time. What can I do to help?"

This is a key message to communicate to the hurting person. Your friend may be feeling as if no one cares or no one cares enough to reach out. This will dispel that false belief. You also don't impose upon the person your own ideas about what might be helpful, but you allow the person's unique needs to guide you. An important thing to remember: If you make this offer, be sure you're ready to back it up, regardless of the time and effort required!

FACTS ABOUT SUICIDE

+ Suicide is the 11th leading cause of death among all Americans.

+ The suicide rate is highest among individuals over the age of 65.

+ Although three times as many women attempt suicide compared to men, four times as many men are successful as compared to women.

+ Guns are the most common method of suicide.

+ Surviving family members may be at higher risk of also committing suicide.

+ Youth (ages 15 to 24) suicide rates increased more than 200% from the 1950s to the late 1970s and have remained stable since then.

Facts taken from the American Association of Suicidology (www .suicidology.com).

Chapter 5

Addiction

Offering Love and Support to Those Who Are Trying to Quit

with counseling insights + ministry tips from
KELLY M. FLANAGAN, PH.D. +
KELLY SCHIMMEL FLANAGAN, PH.D.

It's hard to say when my interest in pornography crossed the line from adolescent curiosity to soul-killing addiction, but I can tell you when I knew it had become a problem. I was a 19-year-old college student, and it was 2 a.m. on a snowy December night in the middle of finals week. I'd been studying for hours, and my mind was numb. I decided to take a break and quickly found myself in front of the computer. Again. I intended to sit down for only a few minutes of browsing lurid Web sites, but before I knew it, it was several hours later, and my red-rimmed eyes would barely stay open.

This was a pattern that would repeat itself weekly for a decade. I remember assuming that marriage would put an end to it. It didn't. I remember thinking that having kids would put an end to it, but they just made it a little harder to sneak away to the computer.

I'd had other struggles in my life, fought other battles, and my church had always been a huge source of strength in facing each one. But for some reason, I didn't feel like I could discuss my pornography addiction with the small group to which I had entrusted my other secrets. We spent so much time during Bible study and fellowship talking about the depravity and corruption of postmodern culture. The women always voiced their opinions about men who objectified women, and the men all dutifully nodded their heads. Including myself. After all, I agreed with them...I just couldn't stop myself from doing it. My friends in the small group weren't the only ones brushing over the subject either. Each week, our pastor's sermon included some list of sins. And I twitched subtly in the pew each time he tacked "Internet porn" onto the end of the list with a tone of condemnation that might have been his or the sound of my own spirit.

So it was that, each week, I sat quietly in the pew, the turmoil inside fueling a fervent prayer, asking for God's grace and his strength to overcome my addiction. And each week I carried that strength with me for a few days, but by the end of most weeks, I found myself in a dark room lit up like a ghost by the cold glare of the computer screen. Each week I felt a little slimier, a little more broken, and a little less fixable.

But then something happened. In the midst of one midnight session, I made another effort at self-healing: I typed the words *Christian* and *porn* into a search engine. The search returned www.xxxchurch.com as the top site. I went to the Web site, and within minutes I found myself sobbing in the dark. Sitting alone in my den, I felt understood for the first time, and I felt the slightest hope of recovery and redemption. On the Web site, I found out that over half of the men surveyed at one Promise Keepers convention had viewed pornography in the week prior to the convention. I found out that, in an anonymous *Christianity Today* survey, 37 percent of pastors reported struggling with pornography.

And perhaps more importantly, I found out that, finally, the church was doing something about it. Churches across the country were taking part in something called "National PornSunday," a program in which every church was invited to dedicate one Sunday to the topic of pornography. Hundreds of churches had already participated. I quickly found my church's Web site and hungrily scanned the announcements. As I checked and rechecked, my heart began to sink once again. Nothing. Not one mention of National PornSunday.

I remember slinking to bed dejectedly that night. But by the next Thursday evening when our small group met, the feeling of defeat had transformed into anger. Hardly aware of what I was doing, I found myself telling some of my closest friends in Christ about my addiction. The tidal wave of confession slowed to a trickle as I felt my wife slide away from me uneasily in her seat, her body tense, her face pale and downcast. I looked from her to the faces of my small group members, hoping to find Christ there, hoping to be like the woman at the well, showered with a grace that compels change. But the expressions I saw were cold and stony.

The first words to break the silence made me dizzy. "Why haven't you prayed about this?" Could a person that asked that type of question possibly understand countless prayers, and would she possibly believe the sincerity and desire with which they were offered up? In a room of about eight people, I suddenly felt more alone than ever. Were the women hugging themselves more tightly than usual, or was that just my imagination? And then another question took my breath away. Words directed toward my wife: "Surely you must have known about this." An accusation instead of an embrace, and somehow my wife was now as guilty as myself.

To be honest, the rest of that small group meeting is clouded in my memory by a haze of disorientation. I remember several other pithy suggestions, ideas that felt like throwing rocks at a mountain, rocks which I had thrown many times before.

I tried for several weeks after that to exist normally within the small group, but the fissure seemed irreparable. After a few weeks, my wife and I decided not to go to the small group meeting. We were in marital counseling by that time, and we "accidentally" scheduled our therapy session for Thursday evenings. Several more weeks went by, with us searching for a new church on Sundays and the old temptation to sit down at the computer creeping into my bones.

I'm not sure if I, or my marriage, could have recovered from another relapse. Thankfully, I never had to find out. One afternoon, I answered the phone to hear a familiar voice on the other end. It was Joshua, my once-close friend from the small group. "Pastor John mentioned pornography addiction in a list of sins today, and I couldn't help but think about you. I've missed you the last few weeks, and I was wondering if we could get together." When I agreed, he asked if we could meet within the hour. So it was that I poured out my heart to a good friend in the middle of a coffee shop one Sunday afternoon. For the first time, I felt embraced by the grace for which I had starved for so long. I remember that he didn't offer any quick solutions. Instead, he asked what had caused me to bare my soul to the small group on that infamous Thursday. When I told him about the XXX Church Web site, he got out his computer, and we went online. For the first time in a decade, I found myself clicking on the Internet Explorer icon without trepidation. We downloaded free "accountability software," and Joshua offered to be an accountability companion. We've met at that same coffee shop every Wednesday morning since then. Rain, snow, sleet, or hail, Joshua has been more reliable than the U.S. Postal Service.

Thinking back, I marvel at how strange it was to have met Christ in a coffee shop rather than in a church. I guess he's wherever we take him. I am forever grateful that Joshua brought him to the coffee shop that day.

WHEN TO REFER

+ **The person asks for a referral.**
+ **The addiction has become dangerous.**
+ **The addiction significantly impairs relationships, including the person's relationship with God.**
+ **The person begins to experience depression or anxiety after stopping the addictive behavior.**

Care and Counseling Tips

THE BASICS

Addiction is a term with broad and sometimes uncertain definitions. In general, an addiction may be present when an individual is dependent upon something and cannot resist the temptation to partake in it: alcohol, illicit drugs, painkillers, prescription drugs, pornography, gambling, food, shopping, or even risk-taking behavior such as driving at high speeds. How do you know if someone is dependent on something? The following criteria may serve as signs that an addiction is present.

+ Tolerance
"I can drink an entire six-pack now and not even feel the effects."

+ Withdrawal
Psychological: "I just can't stop thinking about pornography."
Physical: "I can't stop shaking; I really need a drink."

+ Engaging in more of the problematic behavior than intended
"I only meant to buy one thing, but ended up spending a thousand dollars."

+ Routine, unsuccessful attempts to quit the behavior
"I quit smoking three times this month. And each time it only lasted a day."

+ Problems in daily functioning at work, home, or social settings
"I couldn't go to work twice last week because I drank too much."

+ An inability to stop despite awareness of negative consequences
"My husband will divorce me if I keep this up, but I still can't help myself."

—Criteria taken from American Psychiatric Association: *Diagnostic and Statistical Manual of Mental Disorders*, Fourth Edition, Text Revision. Washington, DC: American Psychiatric Association, 2000.

Care Tips

Your course of action will differ depending on the person's level of desire to change. Identify where your friend is in these "stages of change," and you'll better know how to help.

+ Precontemplation

At this stage, the person is unaware of the problem and resistant to change. Signs of this stage include refusal to discuss the issue, resistance to learning about the behavior, and refusal to take responsibility for consequences. The most effective approach at this stage is to communicate acceptance of the person and lack of judgment. Don't push the person into taking action. Instead, allow him or her to develop trust in you and your opinions, so that when you eventually share your perspective, the person will be less defensive.

+ Contemplation

At this stage, the person likely recognizes the presence of a problem, but is probably more interested in learning about it than in doing anything to change it. He or she may be looking for a guaranteed cure or waiting for "the right time" to stop. The person will often desire change but not initiate it. Your best approach at this stage is to gently increase his or her motivation for change. Increase emotional arousal about the behavior (you might have the person watch a videotape taken when he or she was intoxicated), make a list of statements the person has used to justify the behavior (such as "Marijuana is my only vice and, besides, it's really not addictive"), and find statistics regarding the dangerous consequences of the behavior. Your actions will be most helpful and accepted if characterized by empathy, support, and a genuine attitude of concern. Listen; don't offer statements of false confidence; wait for requests for more information; and calmly report your observations, personal experiences, and factual information.

+ Preparation

At this stage, the person will express, for the first time, a determination to change the behavior. However, the person may still not have a clear sense of how to change. You can help by beginning to introduce useful interventions for the beginning stages of change, such as setting a target date for quitting the behavior, supporting the person's decision to go public, preparing the person for the ups and downs of recovery, and tailoring a plan of action (for example, if the person is addicted to shopping, help set up a budget). Take small steps in all of these interventions. Be aware of three aspects of your role:

1. The person's decision to attempt and implement change will often be accompanied by increased stress and fear. Watch for signs of this, and increase the amount of time and resources you dedicate to supporting the person.

2. Each person will desire different assistance. Communicate openly with the person, and develop a list of things with which the person wants and does not want help. For instance, the person may want you to pray for him or her but may not yet be willing for you to enlist the help of a professional counselor.

3. Recognize that the temptation to relapse doesn't represent failure. Elimination of temptation is not the goal, nor is it realistic. Help the person deal with the painful realization that temptation will always be present. Offer ongoing accountability as a symbol of your long-term dedication to his or her recovery.

—Stages taken from: Prochaska, James O., et al. *Changing for Good.* New York, NY: HarperCollins, 1994.

Counseling Tips

Continue to use the "stages of change" as a guide to the most appropriate intervention. However, as you counsel the individual, you'll be thinking about long-term change and maintenance of the recovery over the long haul.

+ Action

At this stage, the person is actively trying to suppress the urge to continue the addiction. You can suggest three types of strategies:

1. Replace the old behavior with a new one (golf, exercise, reading).

2. Help the person identify cues for the behavior and plan a response. For instance, if restaurants trigger a desire to drink, the person may want to take accountable friends along or avoid restaurants altogether.

3. Help the person alter the environment, when possible, to eliminate cues that promote the addictive behavior: Cut up the credit cards, remove liquor from the home, sell the computer, or cut off contact with friends who use drugs.

+ Maintenance

At this stage, the person appears to have a good handle on the addiction and is ready to replace the addictive behaviors with a healthier lifestyle. You can be supportive in helping the person develop that lifestyle. For example, you might encourage him or her to take a leadership role in the church or in an addiction support group. This may be the most difficult stage to remain supportive because it may seem that the problem is in the past. However, it's important that you don't stop being active. Make an agreement to maintain an accountability relationship (drive the person to AA meetings and/or continue meeting regularly). Offer your support for future times of temptation (provide the person with a number at which you can be reached at any time day or night, or help the person to role-play about anticipated future temptation).

Group Tips

+ Remove cues and triggers at group gatherings.

For example, if someone is struggling to quit smoking, prohibit other members from smoking at fellowship gatherings. Likewise, don't serve alcoholic beverages at holiday parties or other functions if you know one of your members is struggling with alcoholism. If a person is addicted to food, organize group gatherings that don't revolve around food! For example, go to a movie between meals (and *don't* order popcorn!).

+ Provide social support as a team.

Social support may take many forms. The person will be going through a stressful time during recovery, and there are many things you can do to relieve stress. For example, you might offer free child care for 90 straight evenings while the person attends AA meetings each night for three months. You can also set up a schedule for which group members will be available in the event of a crisis. When the person is tempted to drive to a gambling boat, there should always be someone available from the small group to provide alternative activities for the person. There's strength and knowledge in numbers! Network in the church to help the person connect with someone who has successfully recovered from a similar addiction and can be a mentor.

+ Pray together.

The most popular form of addiction recovery, the 12-step model (such as Alcoholics Anonymous—see page 73), relies most heavily on spiritual change. It's likely that group prayer will be a good match for other things the person is doing in his or her 12-step support group. Don't be afraid to validate the person's sense of powerlessness and desire to turn his or her will over to God.

+ Respect the person's wish for confidentiality.

Ideally, the person will have chosen to go public. But if not, he or she probably feels strongly about not telling others and may have good reasons.
For instance, the church has occasionally been less than accepting to people with certain addictions. Respect this wish, and make the small group a
safe place for the person to open up. With your support, the person may
eventually feel more comfortable going public about the addiction to the
church community.

SCRIPTURE HELP

*These Scriptures can help you and your friend as you work together to
defeat the addiction.*

+ **Romans 6:11-14**
+ **Romans 12:2**
+ **1 Corinthians 10:13**
+ **Ephesians 6:10-18**
+ **Philippians 4:6-9**

+ **Colossians 3:1-10**
+ **1 Peter 1:6-7**
+ **1 Peter 4:1-8**
+ **1 Peter 5:8-10**
+ **1 John 1:8-9**

What Not to Say

+ "Addiction is a spiritual disease; you must not be right with God."

Although many people who recover from addiction do find that spiritual growth is a key part of success, it's not fair to tell someone that addiction is *only* a spiritual disease. The hurting person may be working hard on his or her spiritual life, but other factors may be interfering. For instance, early family experiences are often a factor in the development of addiction. People with addiction often have to overcome unhealthy ways of coping learned at a very young age.

+ "I don't know anyone else in the church who is struggling with this issue."

Although this may be true, it's more likely a symptom of something amiss in the church as opposed to something uniquely wrong with the hurting person. In other words, Christians struggle with addiction at rates similar to the rest of the population, so if the church is not aware of any problems with addiction among its congregation, perhaps it's because the church has not provided a secure environment in which to discuss these struggles. By making this statement, you falsely imply that the hurting person is alone and uniquely broken.

+ "If you really wanted to, you would just stop."

This admonition is easier said than accomplished. For various reasons, stopping an addiction requires more than simply wanting to do so. Rather than communicating a judgment about the person, try to develop empathy by thinking of something in your own life that has been difficult to stop, even if it's something as seemingly benign as giving up chocolate. Not so easy, is it?

+ "Only a pervert would look at that stuff on the Internet."

Perhaps you would not say something like this exactly, but the statement is symbolic of a broader issue. Regardless of the addiction, the addict is likely already feeling ashamed. Additional shame from you is likely to drive him or her away. Jesus appeared to understand this concept very well as he opened his arms to people with all kinds of problems. Try to be like Jesus to the addict.

What to Say

+ "If you feel powerless to defeat this, that's because you are. But God can help us conquer your addiction together."

The hurting person is likely to feel validated and supported by this statement. It's validating to hear that one has not failed through any fault of one's own, but simply because the task is not within one's ability. It also communicates the important first step in many successful 12-step programs (see the box on page 73). Finally, you will communicate that both Christ *and* his church body will help the hurting person address his or her addiction.

+ "Is there anything I or the church can do to help you with accountability?"

Accountability is one of the most important functions of a support network. To be held accountable, we have to trust and be nondefensive, two qualities that likely can only be achieved with the people with whom we feel most secure. In a church, that's often the small group. When you address this issue, be sure to communicate a tone of compassion, and make sure your tone is accompanied by tangible *acts* of compassion. In other words, let the hurting person know that your help with accountability will include more than the occasional suspicion that the person has relapsed. Instead, you'll actively engage with them in the process of preventing relapse.

+ "You're not alone."

Addiction can be a stigmatized subject, so the person may not know very many people, if any, who have publicly acknowledged an addiction. Make an effort to share the feelings of helplessness and defeat you've experienced in difficult times.

ADDITIONAL RESOURCES

+ Books

Prochaska, James O., et al. *Changing for Good*. New York, NY: HarperCollins, 1994.

Alcoholics Anonymous. Big Book, Fourth Edition. Alcoholics Anonymous World Services, Inc., 2001. (The big book can also be found online at the AA Web site listed below.)

+ Online Resources

www.alcoholics-anonymous.org

www.na.org (Narcotics Anonymous World Services)

www.gamblersanonymous.org

www.xxxchurch.com (A source of assistance and support for pornography addicts, including accountability software. However, be aware that simply being on the computer could be a trigger, so you may want to go on this site with the person.)

FINDING A 12-STEP GROUP

To find a local 12-step group, check with local churches (many meetings take place in churches). Or write General Service Office, Box 459, Grand Central Station, New York, NY, 10163, for a list of AA-approved groups.

The 12 Steps of Alcoholics Anonymous:

1. We admitted we were powerless over alcohol—that our lives had become unmanageable.

2. Came to believe that a Power greater than ourselves could restore us to sanity.

3. Made a decision to turn our will and our lives over to the care of God *as we understood Him.*

4. Made a searching and fearless moral inventory of ourselves.

5. Admitted to God, to ourselves, and to another human being the exact nature of our wrongs.

6. Were entirely ready to have God remove all these defects of character.

7. Humbly asked Him to remove our shortcomings.

8. Made a list of all persons we had harmed and became willing to make amends to them all.

9. Made direct amends to such people wherever possible, except when to do so would injure them or others.

10. Continued to take personal inventory and when we were wrong promptly admitted it.

11. Sought through prayer and meditation to improve our conscious contact with God, *as we understood Him,* praying only for knowledge of His will for us and the power to carry that out.

12. Having had a spiritual awakening as the result of these steps, we tried to carry this message to alcoholics and to practice these principles in all our affairs.

Chapter 6

Divorce
Helping Your Friend Cope With All of Its Difficulties

with counseling insights from **TERRI S. WATSON, PSY.D.**
+ ministry tips from **JOY-ELIZABETH F. LAWRENCE**

After almost 30 years of marriage, Maria made the difficult decision to file for divorce from her husband, Kevin. Although Maria believes that marriage is for life—through the good and the bad—Kevin had a history of marital infidelity and had not changed despite several years of counseling and church discipline.

Emergency Response Handbook: *How did your church respond to your divorce?*

Maria: The church called a congregational meeting since Kevin was the head elder. Kevin hadn't been attending the church for a while because of what was happening between us and because he traveled, which I'd used as a handy excuse when people asked where he was. Anyway, at the meeting the pastor said, "We called this meeting because we want to tell you that Kevin is under church discipline for moral failure." He asked the congregation to pray for my kids and me and also told them to address all questions to himself rather than to my family or me.

ERH: *How did your small group and Christian friends respond?*

Maria: There were times when I needed to talk about what I was going through, and this is what taught me who my friends really were. I had one friend who was really close, but she totally backed away. Another friend would talk about anything *but* what I was going through. Everything was all "hush, hush" and under wraps, but I didn't really want that. Also, when you're a couple and you do things with other couples and then are divorced, you don't get included in couple things anymore.

I did a Bible study together with a core group of female friends (a different Bible study than mentioned earlier). Those ladies were my support group. They prayed for me diligently, and there was no way that I would have been able to walk that path and go through what I went through without them. I had seen other women go through divorce and wind up very angry, malicious, and ugly.

ERH: *How did you feel being a divorcing—and now divorced—Christian?*

Maria: Well first, there are the shame issues. That's a huge thing in Christian circles. I really had to work through that and was helped a lot by passages in Isaiah and Psalms.

Secondly, I was embarrassed. For what my husband had done, that I'd gotten myself in this situation, and that as a Christian I was going through divorce. Being divorced carries a stigma. Not that when I look at other divorced women I think of them badly, but it's hard being divorced. When you're a widow, there's definitely more sympathy. It's OK to be a widow, but you have control over whether or not you're divorced.

I was angry, too, but I was careful of how and when I expressed it. I know that unwillingness to forgive slides a person into bitterness really quickly. But it was hard. I kept thinking, "This is horrific. This is my whole life. My married life was a lie."

ERH: *Do you have advice for others regarding forgiveness in the situation of infidelity and divorce?*

Maria: Forgiveness is a two-part thing. First, forgiveness isn't about the other person, it's about yourself. You have to let go of the right to retaliate, the desire to hurt him as badly as he hurt you. It doesn't happen all at once; it's a process that comes in stages; it ebbs and flows. There are layers to it like an onion. You get through one layer; then something will happen, and you'll have to peel the next layer.

Secondly, I had to understand that forgiving him didn't make what he did OK or mean that I condoned it. In the end I didn't forgive because of him, I forgave because it was a step of help for me. I told him, "As much as I know to this point, I forgive you."

ERH: *How would you summarize your experience of divorce?*

Maria: To me, divorce is a death. It's the death of a relationship. A lot of people will quote Romans 8:28: "And we know that in all things God works for the good of those who love him, who have been called according to his purpose" (New International Version). I don't believe that the divorce was "good", but I believe that "all things" means the big picture—everything, the bad and the good, rolled into one. It means that eventually God works it for good.

WHEN TO REFER

Most individuals going through a divorce can benefit from some professional counseling at some point in the process, particularly if they have children. Don't hesitate to encourage your small group member to seek professional help immediately if any of the following signs and symptoms are present.

+ References to self-destructive or suicidal thoughts or feelings

+ Isolative behavior

+ Continuous "bad-mouthing" of the ex-spouse in the presence of others, particularly the children

Offering to sit with your friend during the initial call or accompanying him or her to an appointment can ensure that your friend receives the immediate help he or she needs.

Care and Counseling Tips

THE BASICS

A divorce is a vulnerable time for a Christian, but the love of Christ, expressed through Christian community, can make all the difference. The small group can offer Christ's love through competent and informed Christian caring, which involves understanding the many challenges, transitions, and effects of divorce.

Practical concerns—Divorce affects dramatic changes in the person's day-to-day tasks. The person may need to secure a new place to live, take care of household tasks alone, maintain or seek employment, and manage finances.

Restructuring of relationships—The effects of divorce are felt in nearly all of the divorcing person's relationships. Extended family may offer support, but relationships with in-laws can become strained. Some couple friendships are lost because many couples feel "caught in the middle" as they try to maintain friendships with both parties.

Emotional effects—After the initial shock, divorced people often cycle through stages of anger, sadness, grief, and confusion before reaching a stage of acceptance in which they "move on" with their lives. Divorcing parents must also face the task of providing support and care for their children.

Spiritual struggles—Following divorce, feelings of disillusionment toward marriage, the Christian life, and the church often create distance from God and make it difficult to trust him. Spiritual struggles are compounded by issues such as anger toward the ex-spouse and difficulties in forgiving. Some may also feel that God did not answer prayers for marital reconciliation.

Care Tips

The good news is that social support received from others can minimize the long-term damaging effects of divorce on the heart and soul of an individual and his or her family. Caring for your friend's practical needs in a time of crisis is an important expression of Christ's love and will solidify your commitment to walk with the person through the divorce experience. The following suggestions focus on how you—as a leader— can help with the practical needs of your friend. (Keep in mind that it's probably best—and most appropriate—for men to reach out to men and women to women in this situation. Especially for ongoing and one-on-one care and counseling.)

+ Identify immediate needs.

When a group member discloses that he or she is going through a divorce, it's important to follow up after the group meeting to find out more about the circumstances. Don't be afraid to ask about specifics, and encourage your friend to share immediate needs (you may want to make a list). Affirm your friend's courage in sharing those needs with the group, and remind your friend that "bearing one another's burdens" is what Christian community is all about!

+ Be the "point person" in mobilizing the resources of the church.

Churches possess tremendous practical resources for a person going through a divorce. Coordinate the matching of church resources with areas of need that have been identified. Consult with your pastor to identify church members who can offer financial advice, legal counsel, child care, vocational guidance, and assistance in finding affordable housing. Offer to make the initial call to connect your friend with others who can assist in practical ways.

+ Utilize the resources of your group.

You need look no further than your small group for resources that can be a tremendous support in the day-to-day practical challenges of a divorce. Practical ways for your group to help include providing child care, going with the person to court dates and legal appointments, connecting your friend with the local community college to explore vocational options, and initiating "nights out" on a regular basis to take your friend to a movie or dinner.

+ Offer information.

Knowing what to expect when going through a divorce can reduce anxiety, provide a greater sense of control, and normalize some of the difficult emotional components. Connect your small group member with others in the church who have gone through a divorce. Provide your friend with information about a divorce support group in the community. Consider giving your friend a Christian self-help book on divorce, and offer to meet together weekly to read and discuss. Anything you can do to offer information will help your friend tremendously!

SCRIPTURE HELP

These Scriptures can help you and your friend as you work through the difficulties of divorce.

+ **Job 42:1-3**
+ **Psalm 20**
+ **Psalm 27:1-3**
+ **Ecclesiastes 3:11**
+ **Isaiah 43:2-3**

+ **Romans 15:7**
+ **2 Corinthians 1:3-5**
+ **2 Corinthians 4:7-8**
+ **Philippians 2:12-13**
+ **James 5:7-8**

Counseling Tips

Helping the divorcing person with the emotional, relational, and spiritual effects of divorce requires long-term involvement. This is a crucial ministry that can make a huge difference in the emotional and spiritual well being of the person and of his or her children. Here are some tips to help you as you counsel your friend.

+ Listen actively and nonjudgmentally.

Meet with your friend on a regular basis, and make it your goal to actively listen. Encourage the person to express fears, concerns, frustrations, and disappointments. Be empathetic and understanding. Resist the urge to "fix things" or give advice during these times—your task is simply to love! Be sensitive to the promptings of the Holy Spirit during these meetings. Be a good "sounding board" as your friend tries to negotiate the many tasks and challenges of a divorce. End your meetings together with prayer, and commit to pray specifically for your friend on a daily basis.

+ Anticipate and plan for stressful transitions.

Going through a divorce is one of the most painful and stressful experiences an adult can face. You can be a tremendous help by assisting in the anticipation and planning for the many challenges of divorce. For example, what will it be like for your friend to see his or her spouse in court or to meet the new partner at one of the children's sporting events? Talking through these scenarios, practicing the desired response through role-playing, and anticipating times when extra support is needed are ways to normalize and manage the stress of these transitions.

+ Help your friend assess his or her feelings toward the spouse.

The intense and conflicting feelings toward the divorcing spouse are a common place where people get "stuck" in the divorce process. Strong feelings toward one's ex, if not worked through, can result in long drawn-out legal battles, damaging experiences for children, and a lifetime of bitterness. Providing your friend the opportunity to express and work through these feelings can be a huge source of support. Allow some degree of "venting" (better with you than with the children!). Discourage "black and white" thinking about the ex, such as "she's all bad" or "it's all his fault." Encourage forgiveness and "letting go."

+ Support healthy co-parenting.

When the divorcing person in your group has children, consider the needs of the whole family. Children's adjustment to divorce is significantly better if they can maintain good relationships with both parents. Encourage co-parenting, and be supportive of visitation and custody arrangements. Discourage "spouse bashing" in the presence of children. Encourage your friend not to rely on his or her children for emotional support but develop the adult friendships available in your group. Be a friend to the children, and offer to connect them with additional sources of support.

+ Encourage your friend to have hope for the future.

With every crisis and loss, come opportunities for growth, ministry, and new and healthier relationships with God and others. At the right time, encourage your friend to focus on the possibilities available to him or her, and empower your friend to trust God for his or her future.

+ Don't be afraid to pray for reconciliation.

With God's help, your friends may eventually come back together again. Don't be afraid to hope for this!

Group Tips

Feelings of isolation, loneliness, and shame often keep divorcing Christians from utilizing the resources offered by Christian community. Know that these feelings may make your group member seek to drop out or disappear from the group during this difficult time—a time when he or she most needs that support. Encourage your group to reach out to their friend—no matter what!

+ If the couple divorcing are both involved in your small group, keep the following in mind:

It's very difficult for a small group when attempts to support reconciliation have failed and a couple chooses to pursue divorce. Feelings of failure, disappointment, and disillusionment can ensue and should be acknowledged. Group members should be discouraged from taking sides. The group can continue to promote redemption of the situation by encouraging an amicable relationship: treating one another with respect, cooperating in co-parenting, and so on. It's not likely that both members of the couple will maintain membership in the group. Consider making the decision cooperatively about who will continue to attend. Which spouse appears to need the group more? Who is at greatest risk of isolation? Who has the most responsibility for the children and may need the greatest practical assistance? Help the person leaving the group to find another place for his or her own support and spiritual growth.

+ Provide a place to belong.

Offering a place of true belonging goes a long way in combating the feelings of isolation that are part of divorce. Be explicit in your commitment as a group to walk through this difficult experience with the person. Watch out for—and discourage—judgmental or harmful comments toward your friend. Encourage your friend to commit to attend your group meetings. Pursue your friend, even if he or she withdraws. And don't let your friend sit alone in church!

+ Offer a safety net for stressful times.

Sometimes the stress of divorce hits unexpectedly, and knowing there is a safety net of caring friends makes all the difference. Provide an index card with a list of names and numbers of group members whom the person can call when in need of emotional support, child care, fellowship, or prayer.

+ Create a healthy, supportive group atmosphere.

Make sure all group members are sharing their own struggles and seeking support. As a group, commit to engage in honest acknowledgement of areas of sin and brokenness. Be accountable, confess your sins to one another, and actively promote forgiveness and reconciliation of differences. Seek to restore faith, hope, and love within your group. Remember, we can love each other only because God first loved us.

A "HEALTHY" DIVORCE

Although a divorce is rarely a welcome or positive experience in the life of a person, a "healthy" divorce is possible—one that minimizes the damage to the individuals involved, particularly if the couple has children. Recognizing the characteristics of healthy adjustment in divorce can help the small group provide competent, intentional caring as a member faces the difficult transition of divorce.

1. Both parents remain involved with children in order to provide a continued sense of "family."

2. Children are protected from the more negative impacts of divorce.

3. Both spouses are able to accept and integrate the divorce into their thinking about themselves and their future in a healthy way.

—Characteristics taken from: Carter, Betty and McGoldrick, Monica, Eds. *The Expanded Family Life Cycle: Individual, Family, and Social Perspectives,* Third Edition. Needham Heights, MA: Allyn and Bacon, 1999.

What Not to Say

Keep in mind that the worst thing a group can do is say nothing, which only intensifies the feelings of isolation and estrangement. When it's said in the spirit of true love and caring, even saying the wrong thing with good intentions is an act of caring. Here are some specifics to keep in mind.

+ "God hates divorce."
We need to love, not judge. Regardless of our views on divorce, broken relationships happen in the church due to the presence of sin in the world. When a group member is going through a divorce, it's a time to show God's love, healing, and grace.

+ "It's not your fault."
Eventually, part of the process of healing involves recognizing, confessing and seeking forgiveness from God and the ex-spouse for one's own role in the breakdown of the marriage. Balance mercy and love with truth—don't discourage acceptance of personal responsibility.

+ "You've shared too much. I don't need to know that."
Most divorces are messy, and it's important to listen to someone when he or she needs to talk. Listen to the stories, even if it's hard for you. Besides, listening to your friend can help you assess where he or she is in the healing process, and what he or she most needs right now.

What to Say

+ "I don't know what to say."
If you don't know what to say, don't avoid speaking to the small group member! Just approach him or her and say, "I'm sorry about what's happening. I

wish I had something to say, but I don't know what to say." Then, be open for whatever conversation comes up.

+ "Please join us."

After a divorce, many people are lonely. They miss the companionship that came with marriage. Sadly though, divorced people are often left out of social situations because they're not a pair. Don't let this happen! Invite your friend to dinner or a movie. If you're afraid he or she will be uncomfortable, *ask*.

+ "How can we help you this week?"

Do check in weekly with the person to identify specific areas of need and prayer requests, and to anticipate upcoming transitions. It's often difficult for people to initiate asking for help during times of vulnerability.

+ "We live in a broken world, and that affects everything—even love."

It can be a meaningful experience to acknowledge, together, that the brokenness, sinfulness, and grief we experience in this life are so far from God's ideal for us. Some people find it easy to turn to God in the midst of suffering. For others, it's a difficult task to trust in God's goodness. Life on this earth is often unfair, and many times it can feel like there is no justice in the aftermath of a divorce. Longing together for our eternal life with Christ—when there will be no more tears (Revelation 21:4)—can be a helpful reminder of the new heaven and earth in store for Christians.

RECONCILIATION

If a couple in your small group is struggling in their marriage and possibly facing a divorce, try to help the couple in the reconciliation process.

✚ Encourage them to consider the small group a safe meeting place for both of them.

✚ Don't take either person's side—try to be an objective mediator.

✚ Encourage them to seek professional marriage counseling.

✚ Recommend that they try a HomeBuilders study (www.group.com) together or another course aimed at strengthening marriage.

ADDITIONAL RESOURCES

✚ Books

Burns, Bob and Whiteman, Tom. *The Fresh Start Divorce Recovery Workbook: A step-by-step program for those who are divorced or separated.* Nashville, TN: Thomas Nelson, Inc. Publishers, 1998.

Hart, Archibald D. *Helping Children Survive Divorce.* Dallas, TX: Word Publishing, 1996.

Richmond, Gary. *Successful Single Parenting.* Eugene, OR: Harvest House Publishers, 1990.

Kniskern, Joseph Warren. *When the Vow Breaks: A Survival and Recovery Guide for Christians Facing Divorce.* Broadman & Holman Publishers, 1993.

✚ Online Resources

www.divorcecare.com
www.freshstartseminars.org

Chapter 7

Financial Crisis
Overcoming the Insecurities
of Money Trouble

with counseling insights + ministry tips from
KELLY M. FLANAGAN, PH.D.
+ KELLY SCHIMMEL FLANAGAN, PH.D.

February 25, 1997, 9 p.m.

David left me today...I came home from work, and all of his stuff was cleared out of the house. His closet looks like an empty tomb. I guess I've known for a while now this was coming. *Oh God, what am I going to do?*

February 27, 1997, 2 a.m.

I talked to the bank today. I had to sit down while talking on the phone because I kept getting dizzy. Our monthly mortgage payment is $5,000! And that's just the beginning. My car isn't paid off. I have outstanding student loans. Our credit cards are maxed out. I think I'm panicking. My heart is beating fast, my palms are sweaty and criss-crossed with fingernail marks, my muscles are so tense that I am getting cramps in my legs, and I feel like I'm going to throw up. I keep getting an image of myself as a bag lady, the boys in foster homes because I'm not able to support them. That can't be far off, can it?

March 3, 1997, 3 p.m.

At first, I was too ashamed to tell anyone that I had been abandoned, but more bills came in the mail yesterday. I got over my shame pretty quickly. I went to the church deacons today to ask for some temporary financial support. They told me the church "doesn't do that, especially in cases of divorce." I guess I can understand. But why didn't they offer to help me in other ways? It felt like they were blaming me for David leaving. After that, I was feeling miserable, but I went across town to put in my hours at the church where I volunteer as a secretary. I explained my situation and asked if perhaps I could be temporarily reimbursed for my work. Guess what they said? "We don't do that." And again, I have no idea what the church does do. When did the church become so paralyzed?

April 5, 1997, 11:30 p.m.

It's been a while since I've written. Very busy. Moved into our new house today. It's about one-quarter the size of our old house, and I think the boys hate it. Have to get to sleep now. Two job interviews tomorrow...

May 15, 1997, 8 p.m.

The new job is going well...I'm an administrative assistant for a law firm. I'm so grateful for the job—of course, if I listened to people at church, I would have a hard time believing God would help a sinner like me. I keep looking for support in my small group, but they keep telling me it's time to move on. Move on to what?! They never ask how things are going financially. Are they uncomfortable? Can't they see I'm trying?

May 29, 1997, 9 p.m.

I went to a small group for people with financial difficulties today (it's sponsored by the mega-church in the next town). I can summarize the experience in one word: *Hope!* I told my story and saw tears welling up in the eyes of a few people. I couldn't believe it! I finally feel like I've found a home.

July 4, 1997, 10 p.m.

Independence Day! How appropriate! I'm finally beginning to feel like money doesn't control me, but I can control it. I've learned so many important things over the last month. Where to begin? My guiding principle has become this: The money I have is God's, not my own, and I have the simple job of being a good steward of his gift. I've learned some important principles of budgeting from the small group. The first 10 percent of what I bring home goes toward tithe, the next 5 percent to savings. After that, the big things get taken care of first, such as the mortgage, electric bills, and so on. That's the biggest chunk. Then, the priorities get increasingly smaller, like cars and food and clothing. I've even budgeted 3 percent of my income for charitable giving. I'm going to save that money and buy turkeys for a local homeless shelter at Thanksgiving. Finally, the little bit that's left is for my personal "entertainment" money. I even cut up my credit cards! I've also quit looking for another job. The boys and I are able to survive on my current salary, and with only one job, I have more time to spend with them.

August 12, 1997, 11 p.m.

It's been so busy lately! About two months ago, David fought to decrease his child support. I put out a prayer request at my new church (the same church as my new small group), and a church member set me up with a job interview for a higher-paying position. I have never felt so supported. I got the job, and it has kept me very busy. The boys are enjoying the youth group at our new church, too. It's one of the few places they can go where our lack of money isn't an issue. I think they feel very accepted, and that means the world to me.

December 14, 1997, 10:30 p.m.

I really need to share my feelings tonight. I tried to throw a Christmas party this evening for some new friends in our church. It was so *awkward*—I could tell they were all uncomfortable being in my house and seeing my obvious financial situation. I wish they'd have just talked about it! If they would only ask, I could suggest ways they could help. For example, I'm always dedicating my secretarial skills to the church, but no one has ever offered to come over and fix a leaky faucet or to help me insulate the windows. I guess they just assume I can hire someone to do those things, and I feel awkward asking them for help.

December 21, 1997, 2 p.m.

Something happened today that helped alleviate some of the concerns of last week. Bridget, one of my new friends from the small group, called me this morning and asked if the boys and I would like to go with her family to a Christmas exhibit at the local zoo. I was about to turn her down when she said that the exhibit was free and included complimentary hot dogs and hot chocolate. It was so nice for someone to understand my financial needs. She even said they would split the cost of parking with me. It's almost like she read my mind. I don't want free handouts, but it sure is nice when someone offers to help! The boys had a great time with her kids, and they invited us over to their house for Christmas Eve. I thought the boys would burst!

November 15, 2005, 2 p.m.

We were getting out our Christmas decorations, and I found this dusty diary in one of the old boxes that we haven't used for a few years. I thought it could use some closure. I am working part-time now, making as much money as I used to make full-time, and I went back to school this semester! I guess you could say I'm a "returning student"! I guess the truest thing I can say of my experience is that my home is not made of brick and mortar, but my home is in Christ. I'm so thankful for the rich and loving Christian home I have found in my new church.

FACTS ABOUT DEBT

+ **In 2004, overall household debt had grown about 9 to 10 percent each year since 2001.**

+ **In 2002, the average credit card debt among families with at least one card was $8,367, compared to $3,332 in 1992.**

+ **Between 1980 and 2001, home foreclosures increased 250 percent, from 114,000 per year to 550,000 per year.**

+ **For the first time on record, household debt now exceeds disposable income.**

—Statistics taken from *Life and Debt: Why American Families are Borrowing to the Hilt,* A Century Foundation, 2004. Can be located online at www.tcf.org/Publications/EconomicsInequality/baker_debt.pdf.

Care and Counseling Tips

THE BASICS

+ Causes of Financial Crisis

Disruptive life events—Often a person finds him or herself in financial crisis due to unexpected or undesired life events. Examples include the loss of job or inability to find a job (please also refer to *Chapter 8—Unemployment*); major life transitions such as divorce, the birth of a baby, career changes, or a return to school; investment failures such as a stock market crash; and major crises with financial implications such as medical problems, a house fire, a car accident, or a lawsuit.

Personal issues and traits—Sometimes a person will find him or herself in financial crisis due to bad habits or addiction. For instance, individuals with alcohol, drug, and gambling addictions often end up in financial crisis (if this is the case, please also refer to *Chapter 5—Addiction*). In addition, certain problematic habits can lead to a financial crisis, including poor money management or compulsive spending.

+ Effects of Financial Crisis

In many cases, the person's financial crisis will begin in a relatively straightforward way—for example, the person was laid off and didn't have any income. However, as a result of the crisis, he or she may begin to experience debilitating psychological symptoms, such as anxiety and depression. (If this is the case, please also refer to *Chapter 3—Depression*.) Those symptoms may further complicate the financial situation by impairing the person's ability to work or problem-solve in the situation.

Care Tips

More than most other problems, financial crises have a way of threatening our basic sense of security. Your goal in the initial stage of caring for your friend is to protect him or her against the terror associated with financial insecurity. The following steps are most effective if implemented sequentially, and ideally they should be accomplished as quickly as possible.

+ Identify the cause.
Don't hesitate to engage the person in a discussion about his or her financial problems. Most people will be eager to accept help in a financial crisis. However, be aware of the possibility that the person may not initially want to discuss it in great depth. Regardless, do what you can to identify which of the above causes or effects of financial crisis may apply to your friend. According to the person's needs, begin to develop an appropriate plan.

+ Identify immediate dire financial needs.
Help your friend prioritize his or her financial needs, and identify those needs that will have a severe impact on the person's ability to function if not met: mortgage payments, electric bills, or food for his or her children. Try to cut out expenses that aren't necessary, and work on a plan to meet those that are.

+ Pray for your friend.
Don't hesitate to pray with your friend. Ask the person what he or she would like you to pray for. If your friend is too distraught to identify specific prayer requests, ask God to give him or her strength to face the situation and conquer it. Also ask that God would meet your friend in the midst of this crisis and that he or she would use this as an opportunity to increase his or her reliance on God.

+ Foster a sense of personal responsibility and determination.

Regardless of the cause of the financial crisis, to overcome it your friend will have to take personal responsibility for its solution, and he or she will have to be proactive in doing so. You can help foster a sense of personal responsibility for solving the crisis by demonstrating an active approach to problem solving. For instance, you might download an application for food stamps or you might highlight appropriate job openings in the classified ads. Show your friend the practical—and immediate—things that he or she can do to cope with the crisis.

SCRIPTURE HELP

These Scriptures can help you and your friend as you work together to overcome financial insecurity.

+ **Deuteronomy 8:2-5, 17-18**
+ **Proverbs 3:5-10**
+ **Proverbs 30:8-9**
+ **Psalm 62:5-10**
+ **Jeremiah 9:23-24**
+ **Luke 6:20-21**
+ **Luke 12:15-21**
+ **Philippians 4:6-7, 11-13**
+ **1 Timothy 6:6-10, 17-19**
+ **James 1:2-12**

Counseling Tips

After your friend's immediate needs are met, he or she may still be facing a long and arduous journey ahead. The following guidelines are just a few examples of the things you can do to help the person on this journey. Perhaps the most important thing you can do is dedicate yourself to supporting your friend through the recovery—until the financial crisis has been adequately resolved.

+ Encourage expression of feelings.

Your friend will likely be experiencing a range of feelings, such as fear, anger, sadness, vulnerability. Each person's experience may be different. If anxiety, depression, or anger becomes severe or debilitating, don't hesitate to seek a referral to a counselor. The strength of these emotions may be overwhelming to you, but don't respond by trying to quickly assuage your friend's feelings. Imagine yourself in the person's position, and you may be more capable of understanding his or her feelings. As mentioned, when people feel a threat to their basic security, it can be a terrifying experience. Consequently, they may blame the person or entity they believe is most responsible for their security. For many people, this may mean blaming God. Don't judge these feelings. By allowing your friend to express the fear and frustration, you can begin a dialogue about the role of faith in perseverance and recovery.

+ Help the person budget.

Identify someone you know to be a successful financial planner. Get a copy of that person's budget, and use it to help your friend plan his or her spending—or you may even want to set up a consultation with the financial planner. For many people, it may be important to cut up credit cards, as this may be the reason for the financial crisis in the first place. If you're skilled in this area, help the person with the intricacies of financial planning, including things such as consolidating debt, refinancing a house, obtaining a credit report, and buying budgeting software.

+ Help the person find affordable and helpful professionals.

It may be important for the person to see a mental health counselor, professional financial planner, or credit counselor. Do everything you can to arrange referrals. If possible, try to assist with expenses as well.

WHEN TO REFER

+ Depression or anxiety—Some sadness and anxiety are normal. However, if the emotional impact impairs your friend's ability to begin financial recovery, a referral to a psychologist or counselor is warranted.

+ A pre-existing problem caused the financial crisis—If the underlying cause of the crisis represents a chronic problem internal to the person (such as addictions to gambling, alcohol, drugs, or spending), discuss your concerns and refer to a counselor or a 12-step program (see *Chapter 5 — Addiction*).

+ Lack of resources—If your friend appears to lack the skills or resources to recover, and you don't feel confident in your ability to help the person deal with the financial crisis, don't hesitate to refer to a financial planner or counselor.

Group Tips

+ Provide free professional services if possible.

Small groups are often great resources for individuals with various skills and expertise. You can help by providing expertise in your area of training, especially if it's an area of need for the person or an expensive service the person in crisis may be unable to obtain otherwise, such as automobile repair, household maintenance (electricians, plumbers), healthcare needs (dentists, eye doctors), and haircuts. Acts 2:44-45, makes it clear that it's our duty as Christian brothers and sisters to help where and when we can during crisis. More than likely, your hurting friend will be willing to offer his or her expertise as an exchange!

+ Provide nonprofessional services, too!

Your friend may need a place to live temporarily or may be struggling to buy groceries or other basic necessities for the family. Offer your friend a room in your basement or offer to make meals. These services are just a few examples of the little things you can do. Car rides are another example, especially with high gas prices. Be sure to offer your services and time, even if the person in need hasn't asked for assistance. Your friend may not want to be an imposition or may be too embarrassed to ask for help!

+ Help out financially.

Though the most obvious tip, it's probably the hardest to do. With all of our own responsibilities weighing down on us, assisting someone else financially can seem unfeasible. However, if you've prayerfully decided to do so, some suggestions include helping out with daily expenses, coming through for the person at an important time of year (such as giving money for Christmas or birthday gifts or child care for an anniversary dinner), or financial assistance to see a financial planner or credit counselor—something that may result in the biggest return on your investment!

+ Network.

As always, there's strength in numbers. If everyone in the small group explores community resources with which they're familiar, you'll likely be able to identify crucial avenues of financial assistance for your friend. Perhaps a friend of yours is looking for a part-time assistant in a family-owned business, or maybe you know a lawyer who does *pro bono* bankruptcy work. Take advantage of the experiences and social networks of the small group members.

ADDITIONAL RESOURCES

+ Books

Blue, Ron. *Mastering Money in Your Marriage: HomeBuilders Couples Series.* Loveland, CO: Family Life and Group Publishing, Inc., 2000.

Hood, Kregg R. *From Debt to Life: 10 Proven Steps to Beat Credit Crisis & Build Financial Freedom.* Gainesville, FL: Bridge-Logos Publishers, 2004.

Dayton, Howard. *Your Money Counts: The biblical guide to earning, spending, saving, investing, giving, and getting out of debt.* Wheaton, IL: Tyndale House Publishers, 1997.

+ Online Resources

www.napfa.org (National Association of Personal Financial Advisors)

www.onepaycheckatatime.com (One Paycheck at a Time: The No-Nonsense Strategy for Becoming Debt Free)

www.crown.org (Crown Financial Ministries)

What Not to Say

✦ "I wish there was something I could do."
Although this statement sounds supportive, it may be perceived as dismissive. Plus, there *are* many things you can do to help the person in crisis! Instead of this regret, ask, "What can I do to help?" When approached in a caring manner, the person is likely to give you some good ideas.

✦ "You just need to get a job."
Try not to minimize the person's problems. As indicated in the previous sections, it's not always this simple. Besides, your friend is likely already aware of the importance of a job. So instead of this non-specific suggestion, do something to help your friend find a job!

✦ "God must be punishing you."
The majority of us wouldn't be so blunt. However, many people hold a "just world hypothesis." That is, they assume people get what they deserve. Sometimes, the church may be guilty of this assumption as well. Yet, the truth is that people do *not* always get what they deserve. Job didn't, and Christ certainly didn't. So instead of uttering this phrase, assume your friend is someone of great faith, and determine how you can be a part of God's plan for his or her life.

✦ "You just need to trust God."
It's true that the hurting person will need to trust God and his plan, yet be careful not to oversimplify the situation. The person needs to be encouraged to actively seek solutions rather than *passively* rely on God. Instead, ask the person how you could pray for him or her. We could all learn to trust and rely on God even more, but help demonstrate or encourage this trust through your prayers and actions rather than admonitions or cursory reminders.

What to Say

+ "How are you handling this?"

By asking this, you communicate your care and concern and give your friend an opportunity to vent his or her frustration or fears. You can also begin to assess your friend's emotional and behavioral reactions to the crisis.

+ "We can work through this."

By saying this, you imply that you'll be there to support your friend. You also communicate a sense of hope and reframe the problem as something to be solved rather than suffered.

+ "Let's bring this to God in prayer."

With this approach, you communicate something very important: God isn't simply passing judgment on the person—God wants to be a part of the solution. It's important to nurture this assumption early on, so it will become a habit to rely on God during the financial recovery. This statement also opens up the opportunity for intimacy and support in the form of joint prayer.

+ "What are your most pressing needs right now?"

This question has two positive effects: First, you compel the person to begin the problem-solving process by prioritizing needs. Second, you open up an opportunity to help your friend, which is going to increase his or her sense of support and, consequently, reduce his or her sense of anxiety.

Chapter 8

Unemployment
Supporting a Friend Through the Emotional Roller Coaster

with counseling insights from
KELLY M. FLANAGAN, PH.D. +
KELLY SCHIMMEL FLANAGAN, PH.D.
+ ministry tips from CARL SIMMONS

I held my hand over the phone, and turned to my wife Marion. "He wants me to come in Sunday. Are you going to be OK with it if I say 'no'?"

I fully understood the consequences of saying "no" to him. Marion did, too. But she'd spent the last four years watching her husband become a workaholic in his dual full-time roles as managing editor for a weekly magazine and personal assistant to its rather obsessive-compulsive publisher—while she stayed at home with two small children. Her answer came quickly.

"Yeah, I'll be OK with it."

And that was that. Once a suitable replacement was found, I was among the ranks of the unemployed.

We thought there would be no problem finding another job. After all, we lived in the shadow of the center of the publishing industry in New York, and even if the right job meant commuting into the city every day, so be it. It would still be an improvement on the 14-hour days I'd been doing.

That's not how it worked out, though.

It would be another three years before I was able to land another full-time job. Among the employment stops in between: a position as publications director for a nonprofit organization (where I discovered there were organizations even more abusive and dysfunctional than the one I'd left); editor of a fledgling newspaper (which went belly-up after four months); a holiday-season gig as "stock boy" at Sears; some freelance editorial work (which at least kept me sane but was too few and too far between); and several months between each of these jobs of *absolutely nothing.*

But here's the thing: God used those years to produce a very different family at the other end. At the beginning of those three years, we were... well, *really* immature. It didn't take much at all for something someone did or said to set us off. We had, in fact, left our church a year or so before I lost my job. A few months after that, however, we were invited back for the dedication service for their new building. The end result: People we hadn't seen in months—some who were the same people who'd set us off for whatever reason or another—were telling us how much they missed us, and *meant* it.

Once our initial shock wore off, we started talking about going back. And a few months later, we were back in fellowship full time.

From that point, two things began happening in parallel: We grew in fellowship, and we wanted to give back. On one side, people were praying faithfully for us, bags of groceries and grocery certificates began mysteriously appearing on our doorstep, and we decided to join a small group again. We'd been in small groups before—and had even led them at a prior church—but this group was different:

People listened to us "share" (go ahead, substitute "vent" or "whine" if you like), and seemed considerably less tired of listening to us than we felt tired of talking about our problems.

Bob, our group leader, had on two different occasions procured last-minute "scholarships" so that I could go to a men's retreat, which in turn enabled me to have some serious one-on-one time with God and others in our church.

The group host, a fellow musician, had Marion and I and our two daughters over for music and meals after church on Sundays.

Bob also saw in me a gift for teaching. And, despite our situation and my own lack of maturity, he found increasingly larger opportunities for me to use and develop that gift.

And, thus, on the other side, despite our situation and our "neediness," a desire grew in us to give back—both to make good on the promise others saw in us and to help others who were hurting.

It started with small things—playing guitar for the preschoolers, leading a children's group, creating art backdrops for vacation Bible school. By the end of three years, it had grown into teaching adult Sunday school, helping with home visitations, starting a men's retreat, leading small groups of our own, and helping plant a daughter church.

I hope you can see the connection here. There's a very good chance that none of this—none of this personal growth, none of this spiritual growth, let alone God bringing our family into a life of ministry—would have happened if those three years hadn't occurred, and *especially* if our church and small group hadn't reached out to us. We had nowhere to go but God—and along the way, we discovered what his church really could look like and desired to become a real part of it.

Unemployment definitely changes your perspective—and, more importantly, your attitude. Since our hard time, we've seen plenty of times in other people's lives in which they've gone through just awful or debilitating situations. Our "time in the desert" has helped us to be there for others and to be able to remind them (and ourselves) that wherever we are, Jesus has already been there first. We don't need to be anxious or ashamed because he has and will continue to meet us wherever we are.

Care and Counseling Tips

THE BASICS

The loss of a job or inability to find a job can trigger a range of feelings in people. Oftentimes, these feelings go beyond simple frustration with unemployment and may include deeper insecurities. As you care for the person in your small group and implement the suggestions below, keep an eye out for any sign that unemployment has even larger significance for the person. Potential interpretations of unemployment may include any of the following:

+ Failure of life goals

Sometimes the loss of a job may be taken as the most recent example of a growing dissatisfaction with "progress" in one's life. Be aware that the feelings associated with job loss may also be linked to other "failures" in the person's life. For instance, the loss of a job may unleash feelings that have been stored up about a "failed" marriage. These feelings may also further intensify problems with poor self esteem and self-image.

+ Sadness about aging

It's not uncommon to hear someone who has lost a job say, "Who'll hire me at my age? I'm not good for anything." Again, job loss can trigger larger concerns. For some people, this may be a very real concern. For instance, a 55-year-old construction worker who's laid off of his job of 30 years will have difficulty competing with more able-bodied, younger job applicants. You should be aware of the reality of the person's situation and his or her defeated attitude, if present.

+ Failure in a role (such as wife, mother, husband, father)

Be sensitive to the possibility that the person may be less concerned about him or herself and more concerned about how he or she may fail to

103

provide for family (either monetarily or emotionally). For instance, some individuals may fear not being a "good role model" for the kids, and others may feel guilty about not being the primary breadwinner.

WHEN TO REFER

+ Career counselor—Refer to a career counselor if the person is confused about the right kind of job for him or her, if the person appears to have unrealistic expectations about employment that are hampering an otherwise successful job search, or if the person simply can't seem to find a job and does not know why, even after significant problem-solving.

+ Psychologist or mental health counselor—Refer to a mental health specialist when the person lacks the confidence to seek a new job or the person's anxiety or depression is preventing him or her from competently engaging in the job search. In addition, when the person's unemployment was the result of a pre-existing problem such as alcohol, drugs, gambling, theft, or fraud, refer to a counselor for treatment of the maladaptive behavior.

SCRIPTURE HELP

These Scriptures can help you and your friend as you help him or her through the insecurities and emotions of unemployment.

+ **Psalm 37:23-25**
+ **Isaiah 58:6-8**
+ **Jeremiah 29:11-13**
+ **Luke 12:22-32**
+ **Romans 8:26-28**

+ **2 Corinthians 3:18**
+ **Philippians 4:6-8**
+ **1 Timothy 6:6-8**
+ **Hebrews 13:5-6**
+ **1 Peter 5:6-7**

Care Tips

When you've dealt with and contained the feelings associated with job loss, it's time to help your friend begin to overcome the barriers preventing him or her from finding a job. The tips below contain various strategies for making this happen as quickly as possible.

✛ Make a plan for your friend's immediate needs.

The loss of a job has many ramifications. For instance, the person's healthcare may have been linked to the lost job. Solutions to this problem may include helping your friend apply for government assistance. Your friend may also benefit from applying for unemployment and seeking out free professional services (such as walk-in hospital clinics). See *Chapter 7—Financial Crisis* for additional suggestions.

✛ Job search.

When your friend is ready to engage in a job search, don't hesitate to help him or her brainstorm possible job opportunities. Often, a fresh perspective will generate new ideas for the person. In addition, when your friend is considering potential jobs, help him or her to process the various aspects of each job. For example, does the job meet income needs? Is the individual qualified for the job? Does the job match the person's career interests? Is the job and the work environment humane? How do these considerations factor in to his or her immediate needs?

✛ Help your friend set goals.

When doing so, make sure the goals are reasonably attainable. For instance, set the goal that the person will apply for five jobs within a week. An even smaller step would be to identify three jobs to apply to within a short-term deadline. The urgency of the situation will determine the goals. You can be a gentle source of accountability for your friend in working toward these goals. Also, provide positive feedback and encouragement when goals are met, regardless of the ultimate outcome of the job search.

+ Help your friend problem-solve.

If the person continues to have difficulty finding a job, work with him or her to figure out what factors may be hampering the job search. If you're concerned about your ability to help the person with this process, you believe he or she may not trust you enough to discuss these difficult issues, or you find yourself questioning your friend's commitment to finding resolution to the problem, consult the list of possible referrals on page 104.

ADDITIONAL RESOURCES

+ Books

Farr, Michael and Shatkin, Laurence. *New Guide for Occupational Exploration: Linking Interests, Learning, and Careers,* Fourth Edition. Indianapolis, IN: JIST Works Publishing, 2005.

Farr, Michael. *Overnight Career Choice: Discover Your Ideal Job in Just a Few Hours.* Indianapolis, IN: JIST Works Publishing, 2006.

Lore, Nicholas. *The Pathfinder: How to Choose or Change Your Career for a Lifetime of Satisfaction and Success.* New York, NY: Fireside, 1998.

+ Online Resources

www.bls.gov/oco (U.S. Department of Labor's *Occupational Outlook Handbook*)

http://online.onetcenter.org (Occupational Information Network)

www.jist.com (Jist Publishing: America's Career Publisher)

Counseling Tips

✛ Monitor feelings of depression and anxiety.

Many people link their self-worth to their job performance—especially if they've grown up in a family or culture that places a high value on how much money one earns. If your friend links his or her self-worth to the lost job, he or she is more likely to experience depression and anxiety. Watch for this outcome and follow the steps in *Chapter 3—Depression*.

✛ Express acceptance.

If your friend is feeling badly about him- or herself due to a job loss or an inability to get a job, the best thing you can do is communicate acceptance for the person, despite his or her current situation. In doing so, you will begin to help your friend differentiate between his or her current ability to work and his or her worth as one of God's children.

✛ Encourage the expression of frustration.

One of the best ways to prevent your friend from becoming depressed or excessively angry is to provide a safe place to express his or her frustration. If your friend is allowed to express frustration or sadness, those feelings are less likely to fester and develop into more debilitating negative emotions, such as severe depression or anxiety. Following expression of these feelings, your friend may be more able to engage in problem solving.

✛ Prayer.

If you pray for wisdom in discerning God's plan in this job loss, you imply hope and confidence in God as protector and provider. You also avoid the pitfall of implying that God is punishing your friend for something he or she has done.

Group Tips

+ Provide financial assistance, if needed.

Unemployment is often associated with financial crisis. If the person in your small group is experiencing money problems, there are many things you can do to help him or her: See *Chapter 7—Financial Crisis* for ideas.

+ Provide practical assistance in the job search process.

There are many things your small group can do to help the unemployed person find new employment. Some positive actions your group can take include helping the person to purchase career-search software, offering to edit the person's résumé, offering to individually or as a group practice interviewing with the person, writing recommendation letters, and baby-sitting during job interviews.

+ Network.

Especially when looking for a job, there is strength in numbers. The more people who are networking to look for potential employment opportunities, the better. The person may end up working for the friend of a friend's sister's mother-in-law—you never know!

+ Pray.

As the length of unemployment increases, so does the pressure to get a job, which of course increases anxiety during job interviews, which makes it more difficult to perform well, which makes it more difficult to get a job…truly a vicious cycle. It may be helpful to pray with the person for a sense of peace and comfort during a job interview, for trust in God's providence, and for understanding of one's feelings about the continued unemployment and associated behaviors.

What Not to Say

+ "You must not be looking hard enough."

This observation probably isn't true and is very insulting. Even if you want to say this because, for some reason, the person is clearly not working hard to find a job, go about it differently. Help your friend explore the reasons he or she hasn't found a job yet—let your friend come to this conclusion on his or her own.

+ "Oh, you shouldn't worry about it, there are lots of jobs out there."

This is probably the job equivalent of saying, "There are plenty of fish in the sea." The loss of a job is a big deal; be aware that certain positions are difficult to attain and factors such as the person's age may make the search difficult. Don't just write it off and assume the person will easily find another one.

+ "Do you really need to go on welfare?"

It's important that the person explores all options for support during this time. Don't stigmatize government assistance. Unemployment benefits were designed and are most beneficial for individuals in this kind of crisis situation. There's a difference between someone who uses public assistance in times of need and someone who abuses the system. Displaying your biases and negative reactions toward government assistance will likely exacerbate the person's sense of shame and guilt, especially if the person prides him or herself on being independent and industrious.

+ "It seems like you've done everything you can."

This is an obvious attempt to be supportive, but be careful about contributing to the person's sense of hopelessness and powerlessness. You want to validate the person's effort, but also reinforce the need for a continued sense of personal responsibility and trust in God.

✛ "God's got a better job planned for you."
It may very well be true. God is good like that. But this is not a statement *you* can back up. God has his own answers for each person's situation.

✛ "It could be worse."
Yes, it could. But, right now it feels pretty bad. And obsessing over what's around the corner often feels even worse than *that*. Don't disregard or downplay the feelings of inadequacy, fear, anxiety, or uncertainty that your friend is feeling.

✛ "I'll be praying for you."
Not a bad thing to do—and possibly the best thing you can do right now—but simply saying it can often ring false. Especially if both of you know you have no real intention of following through on it.

What to Say

✛ "It may not feel like it right now, but your job does *not* determine your value as a person."
With this statement, you acknowledge that it's all right for the person to feel the way he or she does now. However, you also imply that the person's feelings don't accurately reflect reality. The person may not be willing to hear this from you, but the Bible verses in this chapter may be a helpful reference.

✛ "While you're off, maybe we could use that time to get together for regular fellowship and Bible study."
This statement does a couple of things. It reminds the person that positive and fulfilling actions can be taken during the time of unemployment. It also lets the person know you are willing to be there for support. Finally, it sets a good precedent for a commitment to staying in the Word during this difficult time.

+ "We're here for you."

Say it, and more importantly, *mean* it. In fact, don't say it unless you *do* mean it. In the face of all the uncertainty unemployment brings with it, friends may be the only things a person can count on. And that goes a long way.

+ "I have free tickets/an extra scholarship for..."

With the lack of funds that unemployment brings, the person in question (and family members, too) are likely to pull back from social events they can't afford, and in so doing cut themselves off from exactly those people who might be able to help and comfort them. Don't let this happen. Keep them "in the game." Whether it's a sports event that offers a welcome diversion, a meal out with your family, or a spiritual event such as a retreat or conference (unemployed people need God time, too, you know), be generous with your resources for the sake of those who don't have those resources right now.

+ "I'm going to...Would you like to come along and help?"

Unemployed people aren't useless—they're just unemployed. But they sure might *feel* useless right now. Affirm their value as people by inviting them to partner with you in helping someone else. Bring them along on a service project, on a job (if you have the kind of job that allows that), or to help you work on your, their, or someone else's home or car.

+ "Can I pray for you?"

The flip side of "I'll be praying for you". As needs and concerns are brought up, don't put off the opportunity to pray. Take the time right then and there to do it. And take note of the specific prayer requests—not only to continue in prayer for those needs being expressed but to consider how you or someone else in your group or church might be able to *meet* those needs.

Chapter 9

Rebellious Child
Helping Parents Lovingly Raise a "Problem Child"

with counseling insights from **TREVOR SIMPSON**
+ ministry tips from **JAMES W. MILLER**

The Powers' son, Jonathan, was a challenging child from the very start. In the crib, he would stand up and beat against the bars, screaming until someone would come and attend to whatever need was overwhelming him at that moment. With such a strong-willed child, it became easier to appease him than to contradict him. Discipline seemed futile.

Elementary school was a slew of letters home from teachers and complaints from other parents. While Jon was not afraid to speak out in class, his speaking out rarely made him many friends. When report cards started to come home, they were always filled with the letter U for *unsatisfactory*. The Powers took Jon to school counselors and guidance counselors, but in the office Jon would clam up and give the psychologist little to go on.

The Powers went over and over their own parenting, the things they had and hadn't said. Each of them blamed themselves privately, but often blamed each other face-to-face. When Jon became a teenager, a parent from school, trying to sympathize, told them that this behavior was just how children reacted when they felt overly controlled at home. So Mrs. Powers blamed Mr. Powers for cutting off all debate when Jon wanted to disagree, and Mr. Powers blamed her for encouraging the behaviors they were trying to correct.

Jon's behavior at home soon became lethargic and silent. They confronted Jon about drug use, which he thoroughly and confidently denied. Nonetheless, in a moment of panic, Mrs. Powers combed through Jon's bedroom only to find a plastic bag full of marijuana. Which led to one of the now-frequent family blowups.

They joined a parent support group at church where other parents had similar situations. One parent talked about sending his child to a "camp" in another state. Others talked about persistent counseling even against their children's will. Even though the Powers didn't necessarily agree with everything the other parents said, there was a sense of community—that challenging children were not entirely unusual—and the group gave them some sense of hope.

They counted it a small miracle when they approached Jon again, and he was open to counseling. They had taken a different approach this time—they avoided making it sound as if they were going to counseling "to fix him." They suggested instead that they were having struggles together as a family, and they admitted that some of those struggles were a result of the their relationship with one another, as well as with him.

But in the end, the most helpful person who joined them in the hard work of parenting was actually not a parent at all. Jon's Sunday school teacher, Mark Roberts, took an interest in them and their son. In their recollection, Mark never once offered them any advice on parenting. He just listened. When they talked to him about Jon, he sympathized. He asked them good questions about what was going on at home, but never followed up with simplistic "how-tos." On one occasion, Mark called home to tell them that Jon had been especially attentive in class lately and asked good questions. No reason other than to pay a small compliment. This was the only one of its kind they could remember, and they would remember it forever.

The Powers are now six months away from Jon attending college. Not everything is perfect, but not everything is as bad as it was. It looks like Jon will graduate, and that in and of itself is a great success. They've gotten better about trusting him to be on his own, and he occasionally gives them good reason to. They know that no matter what happens, he will soon be on his own anyway, and the best thing they can do is trust God for his future.

WHEN TO REFER

+ When you believe there is a danger to the child, family, or others—Consult with church leadership and the parents as soon as you believe the parents or child pose a physical risk to themselves or others.

+ If there are issues beyond your understanding or you don't feel confident in addressing them—In a ministry position especially, you may feel a huge need to be the problem-solver. It's OK to say you're in over your head and you'd like some other forms of support present.

+ When you can't be an unbiased advocate for the child and the family—The child's behavior may have a direct impact on your family or be so offensive to you personally that you can't serve them well. In this case, help the family find someone else who will give them the support they need.

Care and Counseling Tips

THE BASICS

+ Understand the broadness of the phrase "rebellious child."

Children who have made poor decisions, who are in trouble with the law, failing in school, getting into fights, or struggling with depression and suicide can easily be seen as problem children. It's important to know that the definition of "problem child" is different for different parents and that a parent reaching out for help in your group is in severe crisis mode. You may learn that their child has gotten caught cheating on a test or is simply talking back to them. Some in the group may think that this is nothing to be worried about. Others may think it's the end of the world. As group leader, you must communicate genuine care and understanding to the parents who are sharing this with you regardless of their child's behavior.

+ The likelihood of it getting better immediately is slim to none.

Most of the time when parents reach out for support, it's after a specific event causes a crisis. It's probably safe to assume that the child's pattern of behavior and environment interpretation has been formed and set over several years. Further, children often act out what they are feeling and experiencing, so it's often appropriate to discuss home and family life with the parents. (Any discussion that questions the parents about their home life should be done in private.) Healing is a process that takes the time and effort of *everyone* involved.

+ Potential symptoms of a "problem child":

Symptoms are often broad and subtle and occur over time. Parents and group members should understand what symptoms to look for. They include: frequency and age-appropriateness of tantrums; ongoing negative behavior; sudden spikes in negative behavior; writing on self and walls; poor hygiene or regression in hygiene; decrease in grades; increase in isolation; trouble finding and maintaining friendships; drug and alcohol use of any kind; cheating; stealing; negative self-talk; too much or too little sleep; increase and decrease in appetite; passive suicidal talk; frequent assaults on siblings, parents, or peers; or any behavior that has a negative impact on the family and/or parent-child relationship.

SCRIPTURE HELP

These Scriptures can help you and your friends as you face the problems of raising a rebellious child.

+ **Exodus 20:12**
+ **Deuteronomy 6:4-7**
+ **Proverbs 3:11-12**
+ **Mark 11:22-26**
+ **Ephesians 6:4**

+ **Philippians 1:3-6**
+ **Colossians 3:12-15**
+ **Colossians 3:20-21**
+ **1 Timothy 4:12**
+ **1 Timothy 5:8**

Care Tips

+ Pray for the parents, child, and family.

After the initial meeting and disclosure, ask the parents specifically if there are any other issues they would like you to pray for outside of the group. Commit to praying for these issues daily, and follow-up with them to communicate your commitment and care.

+ Listen and relate.

It's not your job to fix the problem. It is your job to be the presence of God to the hurting parents. The best and easiest way to do this is to listen first and relate your feelings about the situation second. Help the hurting parent know that you understand the severity of the situation, that you're hurting with them, and that you want to support them through this painful time.

+ Increase ministry time with the family.

You may want to set aside an afternoon or evening once a month—or more often if needed—to visit with the parents and find out how things are going. It may also be helpful to arrange fun nights that involve both your family and theirs—play board games, watch movies, or cook dinner together.

+ Send caring notes and encouraging articles to the parents.

Check out resources that the church may have in its library or that the youth pastor may have available. If there are any relevant articles that would be an encouragement to the parents, send them along with a note.

Counseling Tips

Counseling parents about their children can be a sticky situation. Do your best to understand the significance of the crisis from the parents' perspective. Be keenly aware of the delivery of any advice. Parents may or may not be ready to receive advice about how they are parenting. They do, however, need care and support from you and your group.

+ Understand the complexity of dual-relationships and when to refer.

As a small group leader, you're likely a teacher, a friend, and a confidant. The new situation may have now made you a counselor. It's important to understand that any intervention could put you in awkward situations in the future and compromise some of the roles you most cherish. This assertive effort may have a negative impact on other roles that you enjoy with this family. It's best to refer to a pastor, professional counselor, or other expert in any situation that is beyond your area of expertise or if you feel it might have a negative impact on your role as teacher, friend, and confidant.

+ Celebrate successes.

When children are struggling, it's often difficult to think and say positive things about the child and the situation—making affirmations all the more cherished. It's important to celebrate any successes that you can, even if they are few and far between. This shows the parents that you're still in the moment with them, and it acknowledges God's work in the family and the child.

+ Realize it could be a parenting problem.

Depending on age and developmental stage, children act out what they are feeling and experiencing in different ways. It's a simple truth that coping skills, social skills, and conflict-resolution skills are mostly taught. It's likely that children (especially younger children) who are acting out are responding to people and events in a way that has worked for them in the past.

As a small group leader, trying to tackle this problem can be a slippery slope. It may be best to simply help parents realize that their family system might be broken and encourage them to get professional counseling support. These interactions should be done with gentle care by using *concrete* and *specific* feedback. As you talk with them, be gentle and kind; don't act judgmental or overbearing. Your constructive feedback will be appreciated if it's given with kindness and concern.

ADDITIONAL RESOURCES

+ Books

Clark, Chap. *Hurt: Inside the World of Today's Teenagers.* Grand Rapids, MI: Baker Academic, 2004.

Cline, Foster and Fay, Jim. *Parenting with Love and Logic.* Colorado Springs, CO: Piñon Press, 1990.

+ Online Resources

www.cpyu.org (Center for Parent/Youth Understanding)

Group Tips

Understand that when parents tell you they're having difficulty with a child, they are reaching out in a vulnerable way and there is often shame, fear of judgment, and feelings of failure as a parent. Use these tips with your group to instill an air of acceptance, understanding, and love for the parents in need.

+ Begin a referral and support network.

In any group of people, everyone has experienced pain and triumph. Let the parents know you are with them, and give the hurting parents an opportunity to utilize the group's knowledge and experience in healing. A parenting challenge with one family may be an opportunity to avert a crisis in another family. Have the group answer questions such as these: What are some things that have worked for you in a similar situation? What books have you read that may be helpful? Are there any other people or programs you know about that may be able to offer support? (Examples might be children and youth pastors, counselors, tutors, doctors, mentors, parenting classes, police officers, and so on.)

+ Have a prayer schedule.

Set up a consistent and specific ministry to pray for the family. You may want to form a schedule for certain people to pray each day about certain things. Ask the parents if there are certain things each day that give the child trouble (for example, a gym class on Thursdays or youth group on Tuesdays). Your regular and consistent prayers will be an essential part of the healing process.

+ Organize regular family activities.

Plan regular family outings for your small group. Plan a family movie night, a Saturday of bowling, or a pizza-making party. Sometimes other adults can speak into a troubled child's life as a stand-in parent and say things that wouldn't be heard or acknowledged when coming from Mom or Dad.

+ Help pay for support.

Professional intervention can be costly for a family. Have group members consider supporting some of the help that is needed.

+ Help the group be patient.

If the parents are comfortable with it, keep this intervention on the forefront of discussion and prayer time in your group as an encouragement to the parents.

What Not to Say

+ "It's your fault (or not your fault) your child is acting this way."

It may or may not be true. This is not supportive and is completely detrimental to the work at hand by the group and other counselors.

+ "It's just a phase. Your child will get over it and be fine."

Yes, adolescence is a difficult transition for everybody. However, negative behavior is not just a phase. It could be dangerous, and it alienates children and parents in a way that is detrimental to their long-term relationship. Negative behavior is a cry for help and often has serious consequences.

+ "Kids will be kids."

There is not a set way children are supposed to act. Each person is unique as an individual and must learn to act in a way that's positive to the environment around him or her. Dismissing responsibility with a cliché isn't helpful.

+ "Spare the rod, spoil the child."

Telling parents that they simply need to be more firm (or harsh) disciplinarians does not fully address why the child is acting out. It's never that simple. Sure, sometimes discipline is one of the issues, but it's rarely the only one. And platitudes won't help the parents deal with it, anyway.

What to Say

+ "We understand this is difficult. We're with you for the long haul."

Parents need to hear that they're not being judged and that they're supported—no matter how long it takes.

+ "God is patient and will sustain you during this difficult time."

A true statement, and one that will be proven as God works through the group and parents.

+ "Is there a time you can talk to your child about your relationship?"

This allows parents to talk specifically about their communication with their child, and it may help them see that they should seek out a counseling situation.

+ "I know parents who have gone through similar situations. Can I put you into contact with them?"

Not only will this help the parents understand that they're not the only ones this has ever happened to, it may also give them the opportunity to find wisdom, empathy, and insight into what to do next.

+ "Does your child ever behave differently?"

This does two very important things: It helps some probably very tired parents think about some of the better moments with their child, and it helps them think about what sorts of situations bring out better behaviors.

Terminal Illness
Walking With Your Friend Through
the Valley of the Shadow of Death

with counseling insights from **REV. DR. L. H. CHAMBERLAIN, JR.**
+ ministry tips from **A. KOSHY MUTHALALY, PH.D.**

Life was moving along smoothly for young Nicholas. He'd completed his
college degree with flying colors. Immediately out of college, he'd been
hired by a large company to head the advertising department. He was
about to be married. And then tragedy struck.

It started with a sharp and searing pain in his right leg. A visit to his
doctor and a prescription painkiller ought to have taken care of the situation, but it didn't. The pain persisted and eventually got worse. It was an
unwelcome intrusion into his perfect life. His work began to suffer, and
things began to change for the worse.

It was cancer—a rare form that was hard to eradicate. Nick couldn't
believe his ears as he sat listening to the doctor describe his illness. "This
can't be happening to me," he thought.

Nick had always faced obstacles—and overcome them—but this obsta-
cle...it was so big, Nick couldn't imagine how to even begin. His world
was no longer as it had been. He no longer felt confident. He no longer felt
strong. He questioned God's love. His faith began to unravel.

He remembered the Scriptures he'd memorized as a child, and they reminded him that God would not give him more than he could bear. He believed them, and yet wondered how God was going to take care of all this.

His fiancee, Emily, sought to encourage him with her presence and her unconditional love for him. But instead of comfort, he only felt guilt—was it fair for him to drag her into this mess? He might not even be around in a year—let alone the "lifetime" he'd imagined they'd have together.

Nick withdrew from Emily. He stopped attending church. His work began to suffer. After only a few months, Nick felt as if he had nothing left.

And then things began to change—it wasn't magical or anything—it was just a sort of gradual uplifting. It began in his small group one evening. One of Nick's friends courageously confronted him and opened Nick's eyes to the growing despair that was taking over his life.

After that night, Nick no longer felt like holding anything back from his small group. They became his support group for survival. When he talked with them about his struggles, they accepted him and allowed him to speak his mind. They didn't judge his anger or his hopelessness; they simply responded with grace. And in their actions, they showed him another way...a way of hope. They asked about his progress every week and held him up when he felt down in the dumps. They sent him cards and little notes that reminded him he was not alone in this struggle. They offered to go to the hospital with him when he had treatments. They took him out to dinner to celebrate each little battle he had to fight.

Nick didn't know how much of life he had left to live, but one day in small group, he found himself committing to a new way of life. Before his cancer, he'd been committed to worldly success—defining himself by each achievement, each new promotion. But now, he no longer felt trapped by those desires. He felt driven in a new direction. He wanted every moment he had left to be *for God*, not for himself. He would not waste another second.

Because of the love and support of his fiancee, small group, and pastor, Nick spent those years of his illness in constant pursuit of friendship, God, and a truly satisfying life.

Nick's story isn't finished yet. His cancer is not gone, but his life is not over. By his own confession, he has learned that God works all things for his own good, especially during those times when we can only despair. He now rests in his deepened and more precious than ever friendship with Jesus.

WHEN TO REFER

Your friend will have three areas of concern that he or she will probably mention to you and that you should direct toward professionals.

+ Medical—Your friend may want to change a dosage that he or she is taking, skip a pill one time, or try an herbal supplement. Support your friend for expressing his or her desires, but encourage him or her to consult medical staff regarding those decisions.

+ Legal—You may know a little bit about tax law, wills, power of attorney, and other legal matters, but it's still a good idea to call an attorney.

+ Emotional—Encourage your friend to seek professional counseling for additional support.

Care and Counseling Tips

THE BASICS

Your friend has begun a very challenging journey, and you have the opportunity to be a part of that journey. Many professionals such as physicians, social workers, and clergy will provide medical care and expertise, but the basics of caring and support will be up to you, your small group, and your friend's family.

+ Be a great listener for your friend during this trial.

The old adage that "the three most important selling points in real estate are location, location, location" can be adapted for terminal illness. The most important rule in caring for a friend with a terminal illness is to *listen, listen, listen.* Your friend is being bombarded from all sides—physically, emotionally, and spiritually. You can be a sounding board for your friend's fears, pains, and frustrations. Listen also for the more immediate, practical needs that your friend has, and try to meet those as well.

+ Terminal illness attacks the body like a "thief in the night."

Terminal illness slowly steals the life of its victims—sometimes over weeks and sometimes over years. More tragically and more dangerously, while the long, slow process of physical decline attacks the body, it also ravages the soul. The world will start to treat your friend like an object to cure and not like a person with a life of his or her own. Your friend will start to feel less and less important. Buoy your friend's spirits with encouraging words, comic strips, funny e-mails, and invitations to social occasions.

+ Dealing with your friend's terminal illness will take bravery.

Being with and listening to your friend will take bravery and faith. Bravery because you'll do what many others will refuse to do, things that may be unpleasant and frightening. Faith because you'll need to remind yourself that God will get you and your friend "through the valley of the shadow of death" no matter how difficult that journey becomes.

+ Understand the three stages of terminal illness.

Early—During this stage, the truth of terminal illness has invaded your friend's thoughts and emotions, but the style of his or her life hasn't changed. Your friend can still go to work, go out, and plan for future events. Treatments may begin to intrude on scheduling, but will not yet take over.

Middle—During this stage, the physical effects of terminal illness, either treatments or the illness itself, shape the schedule and experiences of life.

Transition—During this stage, your friend's body fails more and more. Your activities together become less and less. Often this is the time to step back so the family can be alone with your friend. Because you're not family, clergy, or medical staff, you'll probably not be present during the final moments of life.

SCRIPTURE HELP

These Scriptures can help you and your friend as you face the valley of the shadow of death together.

+ **Psalm 3:3-4**
+ **Psalm 23:4**
+ **Psalm 39:4**
+ **Psalm 40:17**
+ **Psalm 91:14-16**

+ **Psalm 103:1-3**
+ **Isaiah 12:2**
+ **Isaiah 26:3-4**
+ **Jeremiah 17:14**
+ **Jude 1:24-25**

Care Tips

People are more than the things or labels applied to them. Your friend is also more than the terminal illness.

+ Discuss new ideas, and do things together.

Help your friend change focus from dying to living well. Encourage your friend to return to reasonable old hobbies and generate new hobbies. Help your friend do something he or she has always wanted to do. Your friend is still the same person that he or she was before the illness, so don't start acting differently. The main difference you'll notice will be the amount of energy your friend has. You still have a lot to experience with and learn from your friend, so use this time to explore important thoughts and build memories.

+ Debate, argue, discuss. Engage in conversation.

Don't feel like your friend is suddenly this fragile person who can no longer stand up to the rigors of conversation. Act as you've always done. If you've always enjoyed a good spirited debate, then continue to do so. If you love seeing movies and discussing them, then do it! The more normal you can keep the time with your friend, the better.

+ Be aware of the effects of the different stages of the illness.

Early—In the early stage, your friend will still want to do, and will still be able to do, what was done in the past. That will include involvement with other acquaintances. Don't be jealous. Share your friend with others. In fact, encourage activities with others that he or she always liked to do before, such as bowling, golf, card club, or movies.

  Middle—As your friend's energy for old activities begins to decline, more and more of his or her acquaintances will stay away. This is when your involvement as a friend will be most important. Make sure you invite your friend to continue coming to your small group. Help your friend figure out a time and a way to still get involved in some activities. For instance, you can invite him or her to golf, but for 9 holes instead of 18. However, expect to have some invitations rejected, and expect to have to leave in the middle of things sometimes.

Transition—As your friend's energy and endurance fades, he or she will be able to spend less and less waking time with visitors. Continue to stop by, but for short visits. Bring a joke if you've heard one. Sometimes just sit and look at the weather together. If your friend starts to get tired, offer to leave, but always say, "I'll be back another time."

ADDITIONAL RESOURCES

+ Books

Miller, James E. with Cutshall, Susan C. *The Art of Being a Healing Presence: A Guide for Those in Caring Relationships*. Fort Wayne, IN: Willowgreen Publishing, 2001.

Westberg, Granger E. *Good Grief*. Philadelphia, PA:Fortress Press, 1962.

Cassidy, Sheila. *Sharing the Darkness; The Spirituality of Caring*. London: Darton, Longman and Todd, 1988.

Counseling Tips

Even though your role is not to be a therapist, there are some counseling realities that will be helpful. The "listen, listen, listen" perspective applies more than ever to counseling as a person dying of a terminal illness seems to rarely experience the same combination of emotions and thoughts twice.

✛ You need to approach a terminal illness with the same insights required for grief.

In dealing with terminal illness, your friend will grieve the death of his or her future. Early researchers of grief suggested that grieving is a linear process with defined stages. We've now learned that the "stages" are actually more "perspectives of the moment." They come and go in a nonorderly manner. Sometimes a stage is skipped, sometimes they overlap or combine, and some stages are often repeated. It's more important to "listen, listen, listen" to determine what your friend needs than it is to try to identify those needs based on a stage. (See *Chapter 2—The Death of a Spouse,* for more information on the stages of grief.)

✛ Understand that your friend might be overwhelmed.

Often during grief, your friend will be overwhelmed by the variety of decisions, experiences, pressures, medicines, options, disagreements, demands, expectations, changes, emotions, relationships, losses, and orders that he or she will have to face. This is not the time to discuss new, life-changing possibilities, but talk about familiar memories, decisions already made, or simply what is happening at the moment. Help your friend find peace by taking time for walks, sitting in silence, reading the Psalms, or listening to music. You can also offer to research information, take on a task, or coordinate a decision already made.

+ Be prepared for an emotional release or depression.

Your friend will experience a roller coaster of changing emotions and will express them—anger, guilt, sadness, obsessive attraction to things, elation, pride, defeat, and resentment. If your friend lashes out and wants to argue with everything you say, don't get defensive. Ask what's irritating him or her. Don't try to defend whatever or whomever your friend might attack. Typically the main thing your friend will need is to scream at something or feel bad for a while. Your job is to be around when he or she is finished. Be empathetic, and try and help your friend make sense of his or her feelings.

+ Do your best, slowly over time, to help your friend accept his or her illness.

Acceptance is not an understanding that the terminal illness is fair or OK. Acceptance is the attempt to figure out how life, both eternal and local, will go on after his or her body stops. Encourage your friend to seek new ideas and discuss what happens next. Exchange images of heaven, and discuss movies that portray life beyond our bodies. You can also help your friend recount his or her life by helping collect and identify photographs, letters, and notes. Or you may want to help your friend leave some legacies for the future, such as a letter to be read at a child's graduation or marriage. During the acceptance stage, what the doctors do will not change much in your friend's life, but you will because you'll be a reminder that he or she is still important.

+ Encourage your friend to "live to the fullest."

Help your friend understand that his or her life is *not* over. There's still time to do amazing things. Take time to sit with your friend and talk through his or her goals and priorities (which may have changed significantly since learning of the terminal illness). Would your friend like to spend more time with family? begin a community service ministry? outreach to family and friends? Remind your friend that he or she is still valuable—God can still use your friend greatly.

Group Tips

✦ Include your friend as long as possible.

As long as possible, include your friend in your group meetings by making special arrangements for time or date depending on the treatment schedule. Once your friend is no longer able to attend your group gathering, send cards or make group phone calls to him or her.

✦ Encourage openness within your small group.

Occasionally set aside your small group agenda, and listen to your friend's stories about his or her job or how the treatment is going. Listening to stories will tell your friend that his or her life is still important to the group. Let your friend know that what is said in the group will remain with the group. This needs to apply not only to feelings and reactions, but also to types of medicine being used or treatment procedures.

✦ Pray with and for your friend.

Keep your friend constantly in your small group's prayers, and, with permission, include your friend's name in your church prayers. If you are meeting as a group and your friend is unable to attend, have a member give him or her a phone call, mention that you just prayed, and ask if it's OK to pray a brief prayer on the phone.

✦ Be aware of tasks that need to be done.

Your friend will be too sick to do many day-to-day tasks such as preparing meals and housecleaning. Don't say, "If there's anything I can do, just ask." Instead say, "May we bring you a meal on Tuesday?" or "We would like to rake the leaves off your yard on Saturday. Is that all right with you?" Be specific. Other needs might be: baby-sitting or taking the kids on an outing, driving your friend to the hospital for treatment or just for a ride, shopping, picking up medicine, picking up movies or books, shoveling the sidewalks, mowing the lawn, or even simply changing a light bulb.

133

What Not to Say

+ "I know just how you're feeling."
You only guess what it feels like to be dying. To say you know is to diminish the value of your friend's emotions and experiences.

+ "All things work for good through God's plans."
God may bring good out of all things, but not all things feel good when they're happening. Let your friend express how "bad" things are feeling at the moment without forcing your friend to immediately acknowledge the good.

+ "Just believe more, and you won't be angry."
This harmful statement comes in many forms—but it always causes guilt and feelings of inadequacy. The worst form of this statement is, "If you had more faith, you wouldn't be dying." And a seemingly benign, but still hurtful form is, "Put your faith in God, and you'll accept this in peace."

What to Say

+ Don't be afraid to use any of your standard phraseology.
Statements like "I'd die of embarrassment" or "She'd roll over in her grave" may lead into a conversation about dying, but often they will just be seen as amusing. Trying to avoid this or covering it up once it's said will only make your friend more conscious of the illness—and will make your friend feel as if he or she is "imposing" on the atmosphere.

+ "It's OK to be angry."
Many Christians feel guilty if they don't accept life's trials with a smile and a cheer. Let your friend know that it's OK to be confused, angry, and

frustrated. God desires open dialogue—God knows the emotions of our hearts, and he wants us to express that. Encourage your friend to "let it all out" and share his or her true emotions with God, with the group, and with him or herself.

✛ "We'll see you later when we come back to visit again."

This is an important reminder that you're not going to abandon your friend when things get tough. Your friend will be encouraged knowing that he or she can look forward to future times together.

✛ "Let's pray that God gives you the time to do all you need to do."

This prayer will help lift the burden of the overwhelming list of things to take care of before someone passes. Be sure to let your friend know that you'll help with this list in any way that you can.

Chapter 11

Broken Fellowship
Overcoming Fractures, Fights, and Feuds

with counseling insights from
REBEKAH KNIGHT-BAUGHMAN, PH.D.
+ ministry tips from **SUMMER RIVERS SALOMONSEN**

I gave my heart to Jesus as a young girl. Raised in a Christian household, I grew up in a solid church and devoted most of my adolescent and young-adult life to mission trips and church activities. In college I fell in with a group of young Christians who were part of a groundbreaking church, which devoted itself entirely to reaching the unreachable. Feeling at home and proud to be part of such a dynamic group of Christians, I committed my time and energy to this church, hoping that God might use me there.

As time passed, I began to feel isolated. I had friends who loved me and who enjoyed my company. Yet conflict seemed to follow me everywhere. I wasn't out to cause division. In fact, I tried to avoid conflict. And yet, my words, responses, comments, and remarks seemed to cause insecurity and defensiveness in my leaders. I tried to "fit in" by not talking, staying quiet—but then someone would ask me what was wrong. Why wasn't I talking? Was I angry? I tried not being noticed in groups, holding my tongue when something funny was dying to be said—and then people would talk about how I obviously had "issues." Many leaders in the church were young Christians, to be sure, but instead of respecting my experience and background, they resented it. They said cutting remarks about ministries I'd once been a part of. They chose to ignore insights I'd gained from my Christian parents and family friends.

I've always been a firm believer in being open with my struggles and conflicts in life. I always tried to share real-life issues at small group. Any personal question and I would answer it, honestly and openly. A real discussion about passages in the Bible, and I'd offer my thoughts. This became my downfall. Looking back, I can see that the more I contributed, the more embittered some became around me. The friends I did have put themselves into difficult situations on my behalf—defending me, my personality, and my abilities—but I saw soon enough that these conflicts would only grow worse and that I was fracturing a once strong group of believers.

I won't deny it: I'm a very outgoing person with a fun and crazy personality—I know I can sometimes come across as forceful and opinionated. But instead of utilizing the strengths I had, my church leaders alienated me. I became the brunt of every joke, of every comment. It was, "Oh, Claire, you know how you can upset people" or "Claire, you need to change." This mantra, of my needing to change, became a sore spot on my heart and festered into a deep seated desire to set the record straight, to confront, and to weed out the actual problem.

The breaking point came one night after small group. I was standing around with a bunch of friends, talking about school and work. A friend, Peter, leaned over and whispered a funny joke in my ear. I laughed out loud, and a few smiling heads looked over in our direction. An up-and-coming in our church walked over, "What's going on over here?" he asked. I'll never forget the insecurity in his eyes and the intolerance in his look. He'd made up his mind about me, and that was that. I responded, feeling like a child, "Pete was telling me a joke," and then added, "Sorry." I apologized—for laughing! I realized, in that moment, that I'd forsaken myself and denied the person God had created me to be. I felt pathetic and frustrated. I'll never forget his reproving comment—full of exhaustion and masked anger: a big sigh, and then, "Claire, you laugh too loud."

I was humiliated! Belittled and put down in a most demeaning way. This situation spurred me on to speak to our pastor, in the hopes of setting a meeting with certain individuals and talking out our differences. Ultimately, however, the mediation was unsuccessful. The tension had gone on too long, and though I was able to voice my frustration, I had no one to temper their rebuttals. They had not come with an open heart, nor were they desirous of rebuilding our relationship. It was my fault, my problem, and I needed to change.

It was several months later that I left the church and moved away for work. Even now, when I think of those people with whom I worshipped and diligently served, I know that this might all have been a different story. The situation should have been an easy fix. What we all needed was a mature leader to address the situation and put a stop to the petty and silly comments. But there was no such leader, and over time the situation festered into an ugly and broken thing.

I see clearly now that the issue was not my need to *change*, but rather our need to *accept* differences within our small group and our church. I brought a strong personality to the group, one to which many were not accustomed. Instead of reacting with acceptance, I was pushed out and pushed down. With the best of intentions, some around me felt the need to change who I was to fit the desired paradigm in their minds. Without reference to the Bible, and indeed without reference to my feelings, they took it upon themselves to *correct* my personality.

I speak now from a place of peace and acceptance. This frustrating experience did not harden my heart to the Lord, but gave me insight into the complexity of relationship. It's my great desire that you might read in this story the pain that I experienced, and promise never to allow that into your group.

Care and Counseling Tips

THE BASICS

Broken fellowship between men and women—and between humans and God—has been happening since Adam and Eve took a bite of that apple. Ever since, we've tried to maintain fellowship with one another and with God in very imperfect and broken ways.

✦ Why does it happen?

Family Influence—A factor of broken fellowship is people's inability to maintain social relationships—something that is established in childhood. A negative childhood relationship to parents (such as abuse, neglect, or inconsistency) may contribute to adult relationship problems, such as insecurity, ambivalence, conflict, avoidance, and an inability to make connections with people...in other words, broken fellowship.

    Small Group Issues—The interpersonal dynamics within your group will influence fellowship—for good or bad. Infrequent attendance; adding or losing members; inappropriate or harmful behaviors such as sexual harassment, sexual assault, infidelity, or stealing can all lead to broken fellowship. In addition, communication problems such as unspoken or unmet expectations, gossip, lies, slander, or individual conflicts within the group can build barriers between people—barriers that will eventually lead to broken relationships.

Care Tips

THE INDIVIDUAL

Caring for an individual who has experienced broken fellowship with the group can present a precarious situation. Feelings of animosity, estrangement, or alienation may make it difficult for the person to receive care from anyone in the group. However, below are some tips for helping you reconstruct a bridge of connection between the person and the group.

+ Take time to be with the person.

Stop by the person's house, make a date to do something together, send an e-mail, or make a phone call. Your efforts at connecting with the individual will serve as a reminder that—while there is broken fellowship in some of his or her relationships—your relationship remains intact. Your unconditional positive regard, warmth, and empathy will speak volumes to the person when he or she is feeling alienated and misunderstood.

+ Respect your friend's wishes for some time on his or her own.

Alone time can be a necessary part of healing from broken fellowship. Let your friend know that you are there for him or her when the person is ready to reconnect. (Don't let your friend isolate completely from social relationships—if that happens, it's time to refer the person to a counselor.)

SEVERAL PEOPLE

You'll face a different set of issues when caring for two or more people who've had a conflict within the group. Use these tips to help you restore fellowship between the members of your group.

+ Meet separately with the individuals who are in conflict.

This is your chance to hear both sides of the conflict. Meet with one person at a time, and allow each person to express his or her concerns. As you listen to both sides, show empathy and communicate care by listening to each person's story and reassuring the person that conflict is part of relationship—and that it can be resolved. Try to stay neutral as you listen and avoid taking either side on the issue.

+ Bring both sides together.

Bring the people who are in conflict back together. Let each person summarize how he or she has been feeling—encourage each person to share their thoughts and feelings with one another. Work with them to help define the problem as well as a solution. Be a neutral mediator, and avoid taking sides.

+ If necessary, call in an objective mediator.

If you feel genuinely neutral about the issue causing the split, you can act as a mediator between the two sides. But in many cases, you'll probably feel sympathetic to one side or the other. In those cases, it's wise to bring in an objective mediator—perhaps your pastor, another small group leader, or a professional counselor.

Counseling Tips

+ Pray.

One of the most important things you can do as a leader, counselor, and friend is to pray for those who are experiencing broken fellowship. Pray that God would use the conflict as a means for strengthening relationship and not destroying it.

+ Work to resolve the conflict.

Gather information—Here are several helpful questions to ask yourself and those in the group:

1. What was the cause of the conflict?

2. Who was hurt as a result of the conflict?

3. Where are the wounded now?

4. What will it take to resolve the conflict?

The answers to these questions can help you define the problem and know how to best serve the group.

Don't take sides—Remaining neutral serves two purposes. First, if you don't take sides, it's more likely that all involved will trust you. They'll feel listened to and cared for. Second, if you don't demean the subgroup or persons who are having the conflict, you'll avoid adding to the hurt and anger already present. You can also serve as a voice of reason when others vent emotion.

Consider the ideal outcome—When conflict occurs and broken fellowship ensues, it's challenging to see that things could be different in the future. Ask your group what the ideal outcome would be—explore together how reconciliation can occur.

Think compromise—Help the members of the group acknowledge their needs, hurt feelings, and desires for the group. But keep in mind the needs, feelings, and desires of the others in the group. Encourage each side to seek a compromise that will work for everyone.

Take action—Do what you can to make the ideal scenario come to be. Help your group determine what is reasonable and what seems impossible.

Call those involved in the broken fellowship. Plan a meeting time. Recruit an objective mediator who has an agenda for conflict resolution—such as a pastor, counselor, or small group leader.

Involve an objective mediator—Have the mediator meet with you first. You can serve as a representative of the group, and summarize the problem for the mediator. He or she can then follow the group through the remainder of the conflict resolution.

Set goals for the resolution meeting—Maybe those goals include a compromise, a management plan, an apology, or forgiveness. Before the meeting, set the goals you want to achieve as a group.

Hold a resolution meeting—Encourage all sides to voice their feelings about the broken fellowship (be sure to give everyone about the same amount of time). Allow the mediator to lead the meeting, and provide him or her with the list of goals you and the group members created.

Debrief—Once the meeting is over, your group may return to its original configuration, change in numbers, or dissolve altogether. It's very important to verbally process the outcome of the meeting together in order to prevent shame or bitterness from setting in. Celebrate the resolution or acknowledge the separation. If a separation has occurred, make yourself available to the individuals in the group, as group debriefing may not be an option.

SCRIPTURE HELP

These Scriptures can help you and your group as you work to restore fellowship.

+ **2 Chronicles 19:7**
+ **Proverbs 15:1**
+ **Romans 14:10-13**
+ **1 Corinthians 6:1-12**
+ **1 Corinthians 13:1-7**
+ **Philippians 2:1-4**
+ **Philippians 4:2-3**
+ **1 Thessalonians 5:12-15**
+ **James 4:11-12**
+ **1 John 1:5-9**

Group Tips

As a group leader, invite the rest of the group to process the broken fellowship together and be an active part of conflict resolution.

+ Examine the situation.
As a group, gather for a self-examination session. Pray and ask God to help each person understand his or her part in the conflict and its resolution. Invite people to journal their thoughts, feelings, and behaviors surrounding the conflict. Present the group with questions such as, "When did you feel most connected to the group?" or "What do you think has caused feelings of frustration and anger in you and in the group?"

+ Confess to one another.
Once the group has taken time to examine the situation, encourage people to acknowledge and admit ways that they've contributed to the broken fellowship, such as participating in gossip or being divisive, people-pleasing, or inauthentic. Don't force people to confess, and don't allow others to point fingers or blame. Simply let this be a time of personal confession—if people are ready.

+ Forgive.
Because God forgives us for our shortcomings, we, too, should be willing and eager to offer mercy and forgiveness to those around us. It takes humility to ask for forgiveness and grace to offer it, but both are invaluable gestures in resolving group conflicts.

+ Avoid gossip at all costs.
Talking badly about each other outside the group setting will only increase the bitterness in your own heart and lead to divisiveness among your group of friends. Talk personally with the people involved or seek an objective mediator if you need advice on how to handle the situation.

✛ Seek closure.

Get together soon after the conflict has been addressed. If the group has resolved its conflict, then this could be a time to celebrate the new depth of intimacy and restored connection. Center the time together around music, a meal, and fellowship. Focus on the new beginning you can have as a group. If the group has dissolved or lost members due to the conflict, then this could be a time to intentionally mourn what was. Group members may share favorite memories or characteristics of the person(s) who left the group. In addition, during part of the time together, the group can redirect their focus and pray for God's guidance in their next steps as a group.

WHEN TO REFER

✛ Dysfunctional family of origin

Oftentimes being in a group can remind a person of his or her dysfunctional or abusive family. The individual's reaction to the group may be rooted in childhood experiences in the first group he or she was a part of—the family. Referral can be necessary in this situation because therapists are trained to gather a family history and help a person make connections between early relational patterns and present interpersonal problems.

What Not to Say

Because broken fellowship generally stems from misunderstandings or words spoken when they shouldn't be, what you should say and should not say is extremely important. As a leader in the church, your position is respected, and therefore your words are heeded. Select them carefully— they can make the difference!

+ "Just act like nothing happened."
While denial can be an effective coping mechanism at times, this is not one of those times. Acting like nothing has happened in the group when fellowship has been broken will only cause the tension, confusion, and hurt to increase. Emotions need to be aired and managed so that resentment doesn't fester in the life of a group.

+ "You're being difficult and too sensitive."
A person's reaction to a group may have far-reaching origins and implications. For example, a person may have trouble with leader-types because he or she had a domineering and abusive parent. Or a person may have difficulty opening up to people of the opposite sex because he or she was sexually abused. Be sensitive, and don't condemn the person for his or her relationship troubles. Instead, help the person see that these relationships can be better than those he or she experienced in the past.

+ "There always seems to be something the matter with you."
When a member of your small group reaches out with a concern, the last thing you want to do is change his or her experience into a personal problem. This comment not only negates the person's experience, but presupposes that, whatever the situation, it's his or her fault.

✚ "Nice try, Jerry, but that's not what this verse really means."

Be careful how you respond to group members who volunteer an idea, thought, or insight. Remember how Christ spoke to his disciples: with love and purpose. Be open to discussion without assuming it's an attack on your authority.

✚ "So, what were you telling me about Bryce?"

Do *not* allow gossip in your midst. It's dangerous. Being someone who doesn't hear or listen to gossip is an easy thing to establish—but is quickly lost with one interested look and lowered voice.

✚ "You know that Jacqueline can be a pain."

When team members are involved in special relationships (spouses, siblings), be extra careful not to take sides. Don't join in when a man makes a funny, but inappropriate comment about his wife. Don't laugh when siblings verbally abuse each other. This will aid your credibility when serious issues arise and you are sought out as a mediator.

What to Say

✚ "Before you say anything else, Mary, let's schedule a time to sit down with Anna and talk this out together."

You must stop gossip! As a team leader, you hear conversations and confessions that can easily poison your mind—well before you go about helping the problem. Encourage your people to restore and rebuild by offering a healthy forum of communication.

✚ "My role is not to take sides, but to foster growth between you."

Don't think of yourself as the great Solomon, presiding over troubled souls, seeking the right and wrong. Learn to mediate by offering unbiased responses that always seek to rebuild what has been lost between two parties. You can create a safe place for your team members by teaching that you are not in one single person's corner.

+ "That was a great thought tonight, Theresa! I like it when you share your ideas."

Be positive with your team members. Kind words and honest reactions go a long way in engendering trust and communication in your group.

ADDITIONAL RESOURCES

+ Books

Bonhoeffer, Dietrich. *Life Together: The Classic Exploration of Faith in Community.* New York, NY: Harper & Row Publishers, Inc., 1954.

Nouwen, Henri J.M. *Reaching Out: The Three Movements of the Spiritual Life.* New York, NY: Doubleday, 1975.

Chapter 12

Church Scandal
Helping People Keep the Faith When Their Church Is Struggling

with counseling insights from **TREVOR SIMPSON**
+ ministry tips from **AMBER VAN SCHOONEVELD**

Emergency Response Handbook: *Tell us what happened in your church.*

James: Our church of the past four years had a long history of *not* preaching the need for Christ as our Savior. But in recent years, some exciting things were happening. I was the worship leader for a new contemporary service at the church. We were meeting every Saturday, and a lot of people were making commitments to Jesus. A lot of new staff was hired who also wanted to see Christ preached and lives changed for him.

Laura: I was working as the director of children's ministry for the church, and all the changes were so encouraging. But some of the church members who had been there a long time *didn't* like what was going on. They said it was necessary to clear the church of the "Jesus Freaks" who were making Christ a "stumbling block" to God. Our interim pastor quickly made enemies by simply preaching long-held church doctrine— Christ as the way to God.

ERH: *So, what eventually happened?*

James: Eventually the animosity at the church boiled over. We live in a small town, and many of those who didn't like Christ being taught were wealthy and well-respected business leaders. They launched a personal and vicious smear campaign in the community—it was the destruction of many good reputations.

Laura: It all culminated in a meeting where those who didn't want Christ preached loudly called for the immediate termination of some of the staff and the return of strict control of the church to the committee they controlled. The end result was that we lost our jobs.

ERH: *How did the church leadership respond to the actions of this group?*

James: The church leadership was totally intimidated by this powerful and vocal group. They met weekly to discuss the problem, but in the end all they managed to do was provide severance pay for the staff who eventually felt compelled to leave.

ERH: *As staff members yourselves, what did you think of this response?*

James: The church leadership failed completely. They were not equipped to deal with this kind of heresy. Many of the elected leadership were newer Christians who took leadership roles because they were excited about the changes taking place. They were, for the most part, unaware of the anger brewing just under the surface.

ERH: *What do you wish the church leadership would have done?*

Laura: The leaders should have shown more strength by stating clearly what the church believes. This should have been done all along so that there was never any question as to the direction the church was going. But at the very least, they should have made a stronger stand after the events took place. It might have saved their staff. Instead, their staff left because they felt at risk of being accosted and slandered on a daily basis.

ERH: *The church was not only your employer but also your family. What were your feelings in the midst of all this?*

James: It felt like death. We experienced a grieving process similar to the loss of a loved one.

ERH: *What do you think your greatest need was at the time?*

James: We needed prayer and fellowship to help us deal with the incredibly debilitating emotional fallout.

ERH: *Were there any small groups or support groups to help each other through these hard circumstances?*

James: The people who came to the Saturday night meeting continued to meet on their own after the church rejected them. Recently, they organized as a home church and have been holding Bible studies and prayer meetings. This has really helped those who found it difficult to move to another church.

ERH: *What practical things were done to help that really meant a lot to you?*

Laura: We were left without any income, and many of our friends took up an offering for us. Their help financially was a huge boost. We eventually decided to move to another community, and they all showed up to help us move. That really meant a lot, too.

James: We have great friends, and it's been hard to leave them.

ERH: *Has any good come out of this situation?*

James and Laura: We began to see lives changed permanently for Christ. Some of the people, we would never have expected to see so bold and ready to lay down their lives and reputations for Christ. The home church that is still meeting is a great example of the body of Christ written about in the book of Acts. And most of all, we never stopped worshipping Christ. In fact, we got better at it. That was the prize God had intended all along.

Care and Counseling Tips

THE BASICS

If we were honest, each of us would say that we're fully capable of making poor choices and messing up many things that are important to us. Many "solid" Christ-followers have fallen to temptation and caused severe damage to their marriages, family, friendships, vocations, and ministries. When church leaders experience moral failure or the church fractures due to passionate interpretations or interventions, the impact is a shock to the community, the congregation as a body, and to each individual member of the congregation. As a small group leader, here are some things to remember if you and your small group face these challenges.

+ Most of the time, the church is blindsided.

When news of the scandal erupts, it will be a stunning surprise for most. Understand that individuals in crisis mode act differently than the status quo. You'll see and experience a great deal of self-preservation at this time. Try to keep in mind the needs of the individual and the needs of the larger church body.

As a small group leader, your job is to have clear communication with church leadership during these times.

+ Factions are likely to form.

As stated above, individuals in crisis will gravitate toward ideas and people that make them feel safe. For example if a pastor has an affair, one faction will probably want to extend grace, and another will want to pursue justice regarding the immediate intervention. During these times, your job is to remain objective, maintain order, and remain focused on ministering to your small group.

+ People are likely to leave, and relationships are likely to be severed.

A church body consists of many people in different contexts. Individuals will interpret what is best for them and act accordingly. It's not possible to prevent this from happening to some degree (especially the longer the effects of the scandal or church fracture are present).

SCRIPTURE HELP

These Scriptures can help you and your group as you struggle with what has happened in your church.

+ **2 Chronicles 7:14**
+ **Psalm 118:8-9**
+ **Jeremiah 17:5-8**
+ **Matthew 11:28-30**
+ **Luke 17:3-4**

+ **Romans 16:17-19**
+ **1 Corinthians 1:10-17**
+ **2 Corinthians 4:7-10**
+ **Ephesians 4:29-32**
+ **Hebrews 10:24-25**

WHEN TO REFER

+ When there is a significant crisis of faith that you don't feel comfortable addressing—Church scandal can cause people to doubt their faith. If you're not able to effectively address the needs of the person, refer that person to a Christian counselor, your pastor, or other church leaders.

Care Tips

+ Meet with your leaders.

It's very important to understand that you're in a leadership position—you're accountable to the church leadership as well as those you lead. Get together with your leaders and co-leaders, and define your intervention boundaries (for example, what can be shared, what's confidential, and the desired outcome).

If you disagree with the way the situation is being handled, voice your concerns and opinions *during* the leadership meeting. The purpose of this meeting should be to seek clarity and reason for decisions and to have an open forum among church leaders to discuss agreements and disagreements.

Leaders should leave this meeting with an understanding of and a commitment to the next steps of the church as well as how to communicate those steps to the people they lead. Unity among leadership is so important.

+ Establish your group as a safe place—a "feud-free zone."

Your group must discuss the situation in a way that honors feelings and opinions. Your group is a place to process and understand—*not* to debate and persuade. Just like you, your group members will have opinions and ideas that need to be aired and processed. Give people the freedom to share their feelings, but work hard to keep the time free from argument and hurtful comments. If you feel it's necessary, set up a time your pastor or other leadership can also meet with the group and answer their questions.

+ Follow up with individuals.

If the group disbands and you think there are some people who still feel hurt or frustrated, follow-up quickly. Give them a call or meet them for coffee, and spend time talking through their hurts and frustrations.

+ Redefine and recommit to your mission as a group.

Meet together to discuss why your group exists. Is it for Bible study? support? prayer? worship? community service?

Celebrate the reasons that have brought you together. Recommit to accomplishing those goals in the following weeks and months. You may even want to write down your goals as well as ideas for accomplishing those goals.

Pray together that God would continue to use your group for his glory.

+ If small group members decide to leave the church, send them off with a blessing.

Leaving a church is a traumatic experience. Along with anger, most will be feeling grief at the loss of important relationships, shared memories, and genuine friendships. The decision to leave is a tough one. Have a formal time to give those that depart a blessing with prayer and celebration.

Don't let people just disappear! Many people who are hurt by a church scandal end up leaving the church—possibly forever. Pursue those who leave. Your commitment to them will help them see that the church as a whole isn't broken. If necessary, help them find another church. Continue encouraging and supporting them as long as you feel they need it.

Counseling Tips

Ministering to an individual or group of individuals reeling from a church scandal or fracture can be difficult. These tips may provide some help.

+ Be available, and project objectivity.
There will be many opinions as to what happened, why it happened, and what the appropriate next steps should be. Make yourself available to help individuals process and understand the situation, but don't put it upon yourself to become a problem solver. Most likely, the situation is too big, and you don't have the authority or power to solve the issues. Call group members to check in, encourage members to speak directly to individuals they are having issues with, and invite church leadership to attend your small group to answer questions.

+ Model open communication.
During times of church scandal, there are many questions and curiosities. Congregation members want their church back to normal as soon as possible. Members need to feel that they're a part of the dialogue and an important voice in the process. Encourage people to address specific issues with specific people. Pray regularly with your small group, and ask God's guidance for your church and your group. Discourage gossip, hurtful comments, and arguments.

+ Communicate trust, patience, and commitment to honoring God.
The situation is ugly, and there are casualties for sure. Communicate the importance of honoring God despite the ugliness of the situation. Remind people that no church is perfect, no human is perfect...but God is—and he is unchanging in his love for us. Recovering from a church scandal is a long process, but as your church seeks to glorify God even in times of trouble, God will bless you.

Group Tips

+ Pray specifically for church leaders and those involved in the scandal or fracture.

Difficult decisions have to be made, and your group has an opportunity to be involved in this process through *specific* prayer. Make it a high priority to pray for those who are making decisions. Pray that each decision honors and glorifies God and that an appropriate balance of grace and justice is applied. Pray, too, that God would restore those who are involved in the scandal or fracture.

+ Utilize the many talents in your group.

Your group is made up of different people with different gifts. In a time of crisis, rely on those gifts. Some people are gifted in fellowship and support, others can offer wisdom and insight from past experiences, and some of your members can offer the gift of prayer. Use your gifts to support one another during this time.

+ Care for those involved in the scandal or fracture.

More than likely, the person(s) involved in the scandal and fracture is feeling guilty, hurt, and alone. Even if that person is gone from the church, he or she is still a part of the wider body of Christ. And he or she still needs (and longs) to be restored. As a group, come up with ideas to communicate grace, mercy, and love to those involved—perhaps you can send a letter, invite the person to dinner, or stop by for a time of encouragement. If necessary, consult your senior leadership before contacting the person(s).

+ Create an album of blessings.

During times of churchwide crisis, it's easy to forget the good things that God has done in the past. In your group, talk about the ways that God has used the church—and your group—for good. Celebrate together the many good things that your church has done. Share individual stories as well as group stories. You may also want to consider sharing these stories with wider audiences (at leadership meetings, during the worship service, and with other small groups).

You might even consider setting aside a time for your small group to make a scrapbook or PowerPoint presentation of those good times. Use pictures, written and verbal stories, and Scripture to communicate those good times. Share your presentation with the congregation or other small groups.

ADDITIONAL RESOURCES

+ Books

Ping, Dave and Clippard, Anne. *Quick-to-Listen Leaders: Where Life-Changing Ministry Begins.* Loveland, CO: Group Publishing, 2005.

+ Online Resources

www.leadershipjournal.net (A Practical Journal for Church Leaders)

www.crosswalk.com (Crosswalk: The Intersection of Faith and Life)

What Not to Say

+ "You know what I heard...?"

Church scandals can be ripe kindling for gossip. Stop the flames before they start by saying only what's necessary. Set a high standard in your group of only listening to and communicating that which will unify and build the church—not tear it down.

+ "I always knew that he/she would mess up."

Not nice. If you knew something like this was going to happen, you should have done something to prevent it.

+ "This church is filled with a bunch of hypocrites."

Theologically, that's probably a true statement. However, a comment like this only produces a need to join the offensive or become defensive.

+ "So, whose side are you on?"

It's easy to take sides in a scandal. But the rifts that are formed can take years to heal. Stress the unity of the church—avoid "us" and "them" thinking.

+ "You're not actually thinking of leaving, are you?"

Some church scandals are of such a nature as to give people just cause to reconsider their future in the church or small group. Let people know they have the freedom to make the choice that's best for them.

What to Say

+ "This is a great church. I've experienced God here by..."

Affirm the church as being a blessing to you and your family by stating specific instances.

✚ "I feel a little anxious, yet excited to see how God is going to mold our church through this difficult time."

Many people and churches have grown as a result of negative situational crises. Rest in the knowledge that God blesses those who listen to him and honor him.

✚ "I'm listening."

Sometimes all a friend needs is for you to simply listen. No advice, no admonitions, just an understanding ear.

✚ "You don't have to talk about this yet if you're not ready."

People deal with things at different paces. Make sure you communicate that if they're not ready yet to jump into a deep conversation, that's just fine.

✚ "I understand that you feel let down by the church, and even by God right now."

People's faith can be seriously tested when a person or an institution they trusted in falters or fails. Reaffirm that it's God who is the centerpiece of our faith—not man. This hard time can be an opportunity to re-center trust where it will never be disappointed.